A MILLION FUTURES

The Remarkable Legacy

of the Canada Millennium

Scholarship Foundation

SILVER DONALD CAMERON

A *million* FUTURES

Douglas & McIntyre
D&M PUBLISHERS INC.
Vancouver/Toronto

Douglas & McIntyre
An imprint of D&M Publishers Inc.
2323 Quebec Street, Suite 201
Vancouver BC Canada V5T 4S7
www.douglas-mcintyre.com

Cataloguing data available from Library and Archives Canada
ISBN 978-1-55365-559-6 (cloth)
ISBN 978-1-55365-640-1 (ebook)

Editing by Peter Norman
Jacket and text design by Naomi MacDougall
Jacket photo © David Trood/The Image Bank/Getty Images

Printed and bound in Canada by Friesens
Text printed on acid-free, FSC-certified, 100% post-consumer paper

We gratefully acknowledge the financial support of the Canada Council
for the Arts, the British Columbia Arts Council, the Province of British
Columbia through the Book Publishing Tax Credit, and the Government
of Canada through the Canada Book Fund for our publishing activities.

Mixed Sources
Cert no. SW-COC-001271
© 1996 FSC
FSC

› Contents

. . .

› FOREWORD

· · · · · · ·

KNOWLEDGE IS the only sustainable advantage in the modern economy.

In the next millennium, the great centres of growth will be based on the creation and distribution of knowledge. They will grow around universities, community colleges, healthcare institutions and research and development facilities. And where these knowledge bases are present, just like an oasis in the desert, we will see a flowering of commerce and enterprise.

Simply put, knowledge is *the* natural resource of the twenty-first century; it is the energy that fuels a nation's intellectual drive and discovery. No wonder the world's momentum economies are making substantial investments in educating their citizens. Indeed, over the next decade, China will graduate as many Ph.D.s as the entire population of Canada.

The benefits of a well-educated society extend beyond economics. They tend to produce healthy and safe communities, dynamic and tolerant cultures, active and engaged citizens.

In this context, the Canada Millennium Scholarship Foundation made a profound and long-lasting mark. But the seeds have merely been sown. The full benefits of this program have yet to be reaped. That's the very essence of knowledge, according to one great thinker: it increases by diffusion and grows by dispersion.[*]

In one sense, that is the legacy of the Foundation. It encouraged a generation of Canadians to develop intellectually and vocationally and, in so doing, strengthened the economy and enhanced the life of our nation. The investment endures.

I had the privilege of serving as a founding member of the Foundation. We were inspired by its clarity of purpose and motivated by the opportunities it would ultimately present to Canadians.

This national initiative was guided by a beautiful belief: that all Canadians have the right to access post-secondary education. For a prosperous society like Canada's, equal opportunity in education should be a privilege of citizenship and an imperative of the state. To be sure, our overall participation rate in post-secondary education is impressive. But the overall rate distorts reality. The fact is that financial circumstance can trump ambition. Individuals from lower-income neighbourhoods and communities have a tougher time entering college or university than others.

That's a tragedy and travesty. Our future well-being depends on unlocking human potential. Canadians must be free of obstacles that limit aspiration, discourage success and divide us from each other. A good education can fulfill this mission. I have no doubt that a million futures took root, if not blossomed, from the Foundation. We are all better for it.

---

[*] Daniel J. Boorstin

The following pages reveal the biography of a fascinating idea. And like all good biographies, this one helps us come closer to the subject at hand and gain a more intimate understanding of the Foundation. It is a fascinating study of character development. We are reminded of the provincial skepticism that greeted the launch of the Foundation—a far cry from what evolved into a productive working partnership. This story is both a testament to the power of ideas and a tribute to those who championed them.

Policy initiatives rarely make tantalizing storylines, but this is a lively, lusty, opinionated account of a truly remarkable national experiment. Hats off to Silver Donald Cameron, whose vivid storytelling connects the large issues of national and provincial policy to the actual lives of Canadian students, teachers and parents. The subtext is clear: good policy is tangible—it makes a real difference in our lives.

A Million Futures is a worthy read. But perhaps more importantly, it's an informative one. There are lessons learned through the Foundation that can be applied to new initiatives. Our continued growth as a nation relies on it.

FRANK MCKENNA

› PREFACE

· · · · · · ·

When I am dead, I hope it may be said:
"His sins were scarlet, but his books were read."
HILAIRE BELLOC

W HEN THE August Personage archly asked me how I was going to fashion a lively book from a story about public policy and public administration, I stumbled.

You'll meet the August Personage in Chapter 2. He's the Deep Throat of this project, a person who has had a remarkable career at very senior levels in and around the federal public service. I dubbed him the August Personage after he made some really amusing and incisive observations about the Canada Millennium Scholarship Foundation and its origins, and then said, "Of course you can't quote any of that."

"Oh, no," I replied. "You can see my little sound recorder. You're literally on the record. You can't deliver these highly quotable pronouncements and then tell me I can't quote you. But what I can and will do is to conceal your identity. I'll call you— umm—the August Personage."

In truth, I was nonplussed by his question, because it had never occurred to me that I might *not* write a lively book about the Canada Millennium Scholarship Foundation. After all, I once won a National Magazine Award for an article about the importance of the potato to Prince Edward Island—and if I could make that story sing, this one should be a snap.

But I should have seized the moment to tell him that I would make the subject lively by finding people like himself—knowledgeable, caustic, dedicated and funny—and getting them to tell me the story of the Foundation in their own pungent words. I should have reminded him that I was writing not for policy wonks or social scientists, but for citizens, parents and students, the people for whom the Foundation was created, the people who are entitled to a clear and readable account of what happened to the $2.5 billion in public money with which the Foundation was endowed at its creation.

The secret to a lively story is always the same: it's the people. Like the story of the PEI potato industry, the story of the Foundation is all about the people: the people within the Foundation, the people they served, the people with whom they had other dealings. It's about their passions and foibles, their frailties and their humour, their aspirations and their relationships, their attempts to wring the maximum value from that brief moment between birth and the grave.

2   It might have turned out, of course, that the Foundation and its officials would insist on being draped in togas of drab respectability. After all, the Foundation was a public body, responsible for an important public function, and public bodies have a tendency to stand very heavily on their dignity. Such touchiness usually means that the people in the organization are fearful and insecure. By contrast, the key people who were in the

Millennium Scholarship Foundation are self-confident and inquisitive. Indeed, they were innovators and risk-takers who considered it part of their mission to foster and encourage a younger generation of change agents. And that fact does make this a very unusual story about change and innovation in the public sector.

The August Personage nods. The Foundation, he says, represented "real public policy innovation. Nothing quite like this had been done before—and it actually did something good for the country, long-term."

Nevertheless, the Foundation was terminated by the federal budget of 2008, which announced that the Foundation's ten-year mandate would not be renewed. The Foundation would award its last scholarships and bursaries in 2009 and would wrap up its activities and vanish by the middle of 2010. As I write this, the Foundation still exists. By the time you read this, it will have disappeared.

So there is naturally a good dash of history in this book, and there are numerous questions and issues—but the fundamental theme is the nature and process of social change—which, in this story, takes many forms. Obviously, simply enabling a student to obtain a higher education is a life-changing act, and the Foundation's bursaries did that more than a million times. Beyond that, recognizing the dedication, public spirit and achievement of students by awarding Excellence Awards to them—which the Foundation did for more than sixteen thousand students—is a wonderful affirmation of individual merit that also allowed recipients to immerse themselves in their studies without undue worry about money. Education is a transformative process, and the Excellence Awards greatly enhanced the educational experiences of those who won them.

3

Chapter 4 focuses on the Excellence Awards Program, which transformed the students who participated in it, but also deeply affected the people who ran it—transformed the way they thought about employment and management, the way they related to colleagues and clients, the way they saw their own futures. Furthermore, the Excellence Awards Program transformed itself numerous times, adding and dropping and altering its procedures in response to the success or failure of its initiatives.

But the changes stimulated by the Foundation go far beyond the personal. The Excellence Awards Program deliberately aimed to alter the country by creating a national network of young leaders and engaging them directly in social change. Similarly, the Millennium Research Program described in Chapter 5 really took fire with the startling recognition that the concept of access to higher education was far more complex than even its proponents had ever understood. The Foundation's research has completely reshaped our understanding of the reasons that students do or do not pursue higher education.

The Research Program's randomized field trials are truly unique in Canadian social science, and they have had a huge impact on the educators, administrators and students who took part in them. The Research Program has also helped to develop a trans-Canada community of student aid administrators under the auspices of the Canadian Association of Student Financial Aid Administrators.

At a more macro level, the Foundation as a whole was effectively a national pilot project in the reimagining of Canadian federalism. Starting its life in a hailstorm of provincial resentment, the Foundation learned to deal with the provinces and territories respectfully and individually. Few federal organizations every truly appreciate that one size really does not fit all; a program that works beautifully in Toronto can fail miserably in Chicoutimi or Prince Albert. The Foundation's approach—being faithful to its mandate but flexible in its methods—emerged as an example of asymmetrical federalism that eventually met with almost universal approval from the provinces.

In a dozen ways, the Foundation changed higher education in Canada. And, at every level, the Foundation changed lives. This saga is salted throughout with the stories of individual people and the ways that their engagement with the Foundation enhanced their self-confidence, enlarged their opportunities and reshaped their lives.

I interviewed a lot of people for this book, and so did Dr. Rosemary Reilly of Concordia University, whose contribution I am happy to acknowledge. Again and again, she and I were told that the Foundation was one of those rare organizations that treated their people like grown-ups. Management told people what they were supposed to accomplish, gave them ample support and told them it was all right to take risks. Its managers accepted the corollary that their people would sometimes fail—but it expected them to learn from their failures and to avoid repeating them. And it got superb results.

"I've read a lot in business textbooks," says one recent business-school grad at the Foundation, "about these idealistic theories on the best way to manage your employees, all about actually caring about them, and having your employer–employee meetings, and really reaching out to your employees—because the number one reason for employees leaving and for high turnover is the employee's relationship with the manager.

"I call these theories idealistic because neither I nor the experienced professionals I know have ever seen them in action. We have basically accepted the fact that they exist in our textbooks and not in the real world. But here, for the first time, I witnessed upper management actually exercising those ideal theories of management, and also trusting their employees and granting them a lot of autonomy. I've seen that when management shows you that they trust your skills and judgement, you perform better and you exercise more creativity.

"It's huge for me to be able to say that ideal work conditions actually exist, and that this type of management actually works."

There could hardly be a more clear example than my own experience with the Foundation. This is a commissioned book, which raises all the usual questions about the writer's freedom and objectivity, but in truth the Foundation's officers gave me everything I asked for in terms of access to sources and people (who spoke to me with remarkable candour), reviewed the book for errors and made no suggestions about my interpretation of the story. In fact, I heard second-hand that Norman Riddell, the Foundation's CEO and executive director, had made it clear to some of his colleagues that he considered it essential that they do nothing that could possibly "compromise the writer's objectivity." He and his colleagues told me that they wanted the book to record some of the major things that they had learned in a decade of operation. They gave me every possible support and then left me alone to do my work. The assignment involved a good deal of pressure because the story is a big one, and the time was short—but the people could not have been more pleasant, accommodating or helpful.

The August Personage saw this as a story about public policy and public administration, and so it is—but ultimately it is much more than that. It is a story about dedication and responsibility, a story about a multicultural Canada that is benefitting from its acceptance of bright young Canadians from every corner of the globe. It is a story about the joy of learning, a story about growth.

In the end, it is a story about the kind of country this is, and the people we are, and the kind of country Canada will become as the next generation takes the helm.

It is a story that made me proud to be Canadian.

> *one*

THE VIRUS OF CHANGE

. . . .

THE TRANSFORMATION of the Babin family of Shediac, New Brunswick, began with an innocent-looking letter addressed to fifteen-year-old Everett Babin.

The Canada Millennium Scholarship Foundation—whatever that was—and the Province of New Brunswick were doing a research project called Future to Discover. Their objective was to learn more about how high school students made decisions about post-secondary education and how those decisions might be influenced. The project needed the participation of a number of students from schools in low-income areas. Everett's school had been selected. Would he and his family be willing to participate?

Everett conferred with his parents, Lisa and Terry. The project sounded interesting. Why not?

The Babins learned that Future to Discover—or F2D, as it became known—would divide its student participants at random into four groups. One group would be given extensive

9

counselling about careers and educational options. A second group would be given a purely financial incentive: a scholarship account into which $2,000 would be deposited when the student completed Grade 10, another $2,000 after Grade 11 and $4,000 on graduation—a total of $8,000 to be applied towards post-secondary education. The third group would receive both the counselling and a scholarship. The fourth group—the control group—would simply receive an annual phone call checking up on their educational progress. The researchers would note which group was most likely to go on to post-secondary study.

Everett was assigned to the third group. He'd be receiving both the counselling and the scholarship.

The Grade 10 F2D program, called Career Focusing, started with a tight focus on the thirty students in the workshop as unique individuals. At his core, who was Everett Babin? What did he like to do? What did he do well? Was he a planner or a plunger, a persuader or a discoverer? How did he like to work—alone or with others?

Armed with this new self-awareness, the students researched careers that matched their personalities and talents. They learned about job shadowing, interviewing, site visits, online research. Everett had been thinking that he'd like to be a pharmacist, like his uncle who worked at the hospital in Campbellton. On further reflection, he wasn't so sure.

"Pharmacy was a really exciting field to be in," he says, "but you really had to have your sciences down, and you had to go to university for six years, and I didn't really feel like getting into hundreds of thousands of dollars of debt just so I could work in a hospital. And I wasn't really sure I wanted to do it for the rest of my life."

Instead, he remembered the joy he'd found in dismantling the engine of an old Subaru and rebuilding it successfully. He didn't think he wanted to be a mechanic, but maybe he wanted to do something that involved problem solving and physical work as well as mental challenge.

Throughout the program, the professional facilitators and educators were joined by "post-secondary ambassadors" or PSAS—students enrolled in post-secondary programs who could give the high-schoolers a real-world understanding of just what higher education was actually like. The counselling sessions demystified higher education, reassured participants about their abilities and introduced them to such topics as time management, setting priorities, budgeting, study skills and learning styles. Throughout, they encouraged participants to be flexible, attentive and open to change.

"I love it," says Laura Davidson, a PSA who's studying commerce at Mount Allison University. "Counsellors don't have time to do all this, and parents don't know this stuff. We were all in that situation once; we were all struggling and trying to figure out what we were going to do with our lives. It's a big scary question; it really is. And we could tell them it's okay, it's really not that big of a deal. If you don't want to go to school right now, you don't have to. If you don't know what you want to do, we're here to help you figure it out."

Everett stayed with the program through Grade 12, when the sessions focused on resiliency and coping with life transitions. When he graduated from high school in 2007, he decided to attend Holland College in Prince Edward Island to become a plumber. But the big transition in the Babin family stemmed from the Future to Discover Program in Grade 11. That year's program was called Lasting Gifts, and it included several evening workshops with parents. So Lisa and Terry Babin attended along with Everett.

The reason for parents' participation, explains F2D's Lisa Calhoun, is that they "are the number one influence, and often they have very set ideas about students' futures and what success would be. So we tried to open the minds of the parents, to remind them that there are four streams of post-secondary education—not only university, but also community college, private vocational institutes and apprenticeships. And any of those could be valuable, depending on the child and his or her strengths. We stressed the changing nature of work, and the ways that young people can develop marketable skills. We talked about volunteerism, time management, networking, ways to research different occupations.

"And we had the parents share their experiences, too. It turned out that a lot of them hadn't thought much about their own careers before starting out, and a lot of them enjoyed the discussion as much or more than their children. We found we were starting conversations within the family."

Indeed they were. On the way home in the car, Lisa drove and Everett sat beside her. Terry sat in the back. Lisa and Everett talked about what had happened that evening, what they had learned, and that, says Everett, "was when Mom's wheels started to turn as well."

"I was sitting back observing," Terry remembers. "I could see that what Everett was saying was motivating Lisa, and what Lisa was saying was motivating Everett. It was really neat to see that whole chemistry happening."

And Lisa was indeed reconsidering her whole future.

"As adults, we tend to think we don't have a future," says Lisa. "We tend to think that wherever we are, this *is* our future.

I'd been twelve years in a dead-end office job, working for a soft-drink manufacturing company. There was no chance for advancement, no chance for any learning. And just listening to the program and what Everett was coming home with—it planted that seed. If I'm going to be happy, now and in my future, I'm the one that's got to take steps to make that happen."

As it happens, Lisa's parents are federal civil servants, and she knew exactly what her ideal job would be: working in the pension-administration offices of Public Works and Government Services Canada, which are located in Shediac. But she'd always considered those jobs to be plums that were well out of her reach.

Future to Discover changed all that.

"I just thought, hell, yes, I can do this," she remembers, with a laugh. "I've got twelve years of experience in an office, for instance—that's got to be worth something. It was a matter of looking at what I had to offer, and seeing that it had value." She applied, and then went through a full year of tests, examinations and interviews.

"When I was called in for interviews, I made good and sure I was ready," she remembers. "Some of the things that Everett had learned were about interviews—how do you present yourself, and how do you present your material? You don't show up in a ratty pair of jeans and a stained T-shirt, with a coffee-stained copy of your wrinkled resumé. You put some effort in, you learn about who you're talking to. Every time I went in, I had my resumé, I had my name on top, I had my photo ID, I had my licence, I had my diploma, everything and anything that I had that I thought would be of value, all in page protectors, and I gave that to them."

And she got the job.

In the meantime, Terry had been watching Lisa's progress—and musing about what he'd overheard from the back seat.

"I originally was trained in computers," Terry explains, "and was working for a company that unfortunately went out of business. I got laid off, and I couldn't find anything in the computer field. Construction's in my background, so I took a job as install coordinator with Home Depot, which had nothing to do with computers.

"But whenever we had an order to be shipped, I had to contact someone at Armour Transportation, and after a year and a half someone I'd met at Armour called me up and said, 'Listen, you seem to be pretty good with computers and stuff, and we've got a job here you might be interested in.' So I went for an interview—and I got the job the next day."

"And that's something they talked about at the sessions," says Lisa. "About networking, about how everything's connected."

"Yeah," nods Terry. "I was *safe* at Home Depot, you know? But this course—just sitting in on it once in a while, you start thinking: Maybe I'm not as stuck in this rut as I thought I was. And now I'm lucky enough to be back in a field that I really enjoy, and in a company where you're treated like family." Armour Transportation, in fact, has been honoured as one of Canada's 50 Best Managed Companies.

Future to Discover, says Terry, "seemed to understand that there are all kinds of different kids out there, who learn differently and have different interests." The provincial Minister of Education at the time was Kelly Lamrock, and he asked Terry, as a parent, what he thought of the program. "I told him that the last four years of education need to have more programs like this, to get the juices flowing, to prepare kids for the future. Because it's what's needed to keep our world moving."

The Department of Education must have listened. The original Future to Discover experiment, funded by the Canada Millennium Scholarship Foundation, has finished, but elements of it are still operating in the schools of New Brunswick.

And all three Babins are happy in their work.

THE TRANSFORMATION of the Babin family is a remarkable story—with a remarkable origin.

The Canada Millennium Scholarship Foundation was created by the Government of Canada in 1998. It was designed to change the life circumstances of post-secondary students, not to change the vocations of their parents. But once the virus of change is set loose, it's impossible to predict where it will go.

The mission of the Foundation was to distribute a $2.5-billion endowment over a ten-year mandate, 95 per cent of it in the form of bursaries, and up to 5 per cent as merit-based scholarships. During the first ten years of the new millennium, the Foundation was to provide 100,000 bursaries and scholarships annually to Canadian students pursuing post-secondary education. It did that, too.

That's a million scholarships. A million futures.

The money came from the federal government's first surplus budget after nearly a decade of spending cuts and fiscal restraints. The purpose of the Foundation was to celebrate the arrival of the millennium in the year 2000 by investing in the minds, ambitions and spirits of young Canadians. And its champion was the Right Honourable Jean Chrétien, the Prime Minister of Canada.

"When the millennium arrived, we were debating within the government, what should we do?" Chrétien later reflected. "The millennium, it's something that comes only every one thousand

15

years—so the next one, we might not be here. We discussed it, and we concluded that we would create a *programme de bourses,* a bursary program. We would invest in the brains of the young people. And when I see the results today, that decision gives me a lot of satisfaction."

"It's true, the impetus for this program came directly from Prime Minister Chrétien," says Norman Riddell, the Foundation's CEO and executive director. "Mr. Chrétien was born into a family of modest means, with a lot of children. His parents cared very much about higher education, though, and they made a lot of sacrifices for their children's education. They even quit smoking, for instance, and put the savings into an education fund.

"Mr. Chrétien felt that higher education had given him a chance that he would never have had otherwise, and he wanted to provide other young people with similar opportunities. That's why the legislation that established this Foundation specified that its purpose was 'to improve access to post-secondary education in Canada.'"

That sounds straightforward. And the Foundation would improve access, presumably, by providing financial support to students in need. Simple.

Except it wasn't. How do you determine a student's level of need? By his or her level of debt? It turned out that students from middle-class families were relatively comfortable taking on debt, while students from less prosperous families were wary of it. If you assessed need by levels of debt, you'd be providing funds to middle-class students, not to students like some at the University College of Cape Breton (UCCB), where I taught in the mid-1990s. UCCB (now Cape Breton University) was the most desperately underfunded institution in Canada, serving a community whose sustaining industries—steel, coal, fishing—had all collapsed. Although most UCCB students had been forced to take out loans, they hated debt and would go to great lengths to minimize it. Some of them combined work and study during the day, napped in the evenings and then spent the night as security guards or hotel desk clerks. A few of them lived in their cars.

If you measure need by debt, you may miss the night clerk or the student asleep in the car—the ones most in need of assistance. But if student debt is not, by itself, an adequate measure of need, what is? What does "access" mean, and how do you improve it? Are you improving access by giving money to students who are already enrolled in higher education? Yes, those students may be struggling, and they may be accumulating heavy burdens of debt. But they don't have an access problem. They are convinced of the value of post-secondary education, and they have managed to get into the system. Financial assistance to currently enrolled students does address the question of persistence, which the Foundation ultimately came to see as an aspect of access. But the people who truly do not have access to the system are, by definition, those who are *not* enrolled.

Looking for answers, the Foundation reviewed the existing research. It soon discovered that very little research had been done on student aid and access to post-secondary education in Canada. To meet its own mandate, the Foundation would have to do its own research.

The Foundation's research soon indicated that programs designed to significantly improve access to higher education would have to start far upstream, in high school or earlier, and would need to affect the way teenagers thought about themselves, about their futures, about debt and the financial return on an educational investment, about the very idea of pursuing post-secondary learning. Or so it seemed in theory. But was it possible to test that theory in real life? Could the Foundation organize a set of experiments designed to identify techniques that would motivate young people to proceed to post-secondary education and to persist at it?

The Foundation's research team designed a series of pilot projects calculated to test the effectiveness of various means of motivating students to proceed to higher education. The projects would provide academic, informational, social and financial support to actual high school students in real schools, and would compare their levels of enrollment in post-secondary programs to control groups of comparable students who had not received such support. The school systems, however, fall within the provinces' jealously guarded jurisdiction over education. So the pilot projects could only be developed and tested in partnership with the provinces. Fortunately, the Foundation had overcome some serious initial difficulties with the provinces—and the provinces became willing partners.

"We're very proud of the relationships we've established with the provinces," says Norman Riddell. "We think that those relationships have produced programs that have important and positive effects on students. Those programs change the way that young people think about the future and the likelihood that they'll 'acquire the knowledge and skills they need to participate in a changing economy and society,' to quote the language of the Act that created us."

One such pilot project was the Future to Discover Program— the program that enlisted fifteen-year-old Everett Babin of Shediac, New Brunswick. And that's how Lisa and Terry Babin were motivated to change their lives.

IT'S A long way from that first budget surplus, in 1998, and the idea of a *programme de bourse*, to the story of the Babins.

In a remarkably organic way, the Foundation grew, branched and evolved in response to its deepening understanding of the implications of its mandate: to address the growing problem of student debt and to improve access to higher education.

Debt had become a major disincentive for potential students, driven by a shortage of jobs for graduates due to the recession of the early 1990s and a wave of government cutbacks. In addition, the job market was clogged with baby boomers, the oldest of whom were still at least fifteen years from retirement. To the young adult of the 1990s, the calculation was obvious. If I go to college, I'll graduate with a huge mortgage on my life, and I won't even be assured of a decent job. Why would I do that? Higher education is a dumb investment.

The Foundation did alleviate the debt problem, although student indebtedness remains a real concern. In early 2009, as the Foundation was winding down, the Canadian Federation of Students estimated that Canadian students owed $13 billion to the federal government alone, not counting what they owed to provincial governments, banks, credit card issuers, families and other lenders. And the amount was growing by $1.2 million every single day.

At one level, student debt is a very personal problem. As one parent remarked at a graduation ceremony, "It's good my daughter has a degree, but who's going to marry her now? She comes with a $40,000 debt. Can she ever afford to have children?" Education was leaving a hangover of debt and repayment that hobbled graduates into middle age.

At another level, however, student debt is a national problem. When high costs and heavy debt prevent bright young people from fully developing their skills and talents, the country suffers as well as the individual. Canada's economy is still dominated by resource industries, but jobs in those industries are dwindling,

19

while information-economy jobs are expanding both in numbers and in influence. The mill hand is literally being replaced by the process-control computer tended by an information technology graduate. In the new millennium, Canada doesn't need many loggers and miners, but it does need engineers, environmental entrepreneurs, film editors, product designers, artists, software developers, biotech researchers, financial analysts and the like. Post-secondary education is crucial to the country's competitiveness and to our capacity to create and retain the enterprises of the future.

So the argument for a federal initiative in the field of student aid was a powerful one. But it came with two political problems.

The first was the issue of jurisdiction, the certainty that at least some of the provinces would see any initiative in the field of student aid as an invasion of their constitutional terrain. In addition, the federal government had just vanquished its budget deficit in part on the backs of the provinces—or so the provinces felt. Dealing with provincial objections would therefore require considerable diplomacy, although the Foundation would also enjoy the traditional federal advantage of having a lot of money available to spend on an issue of great concern to the provinces. Both sides would be well motivated to reach an accord.

The other political problem was related to the federal budget. Having just eliminated the deficit, the government was not eager to increase its annual financial commitments by starting a program that would have to be funded every year from current revenues. But a one-time expenditure—an endowment—would neatly sidestep that issue.

The millennium provided the opportunity. Every government in the world was planning memorials, celebrations, monuments. The British, for instance, were erecting a fancy building on the banks of the Thames, the Millennium Dome, at a cost of $1.3 billion.

How would Canada commemorate the millennium? With a *programme de bourses,* a bursary and scholarship program housed in a private, free-standing foundation endowed by a single, substantial injection of cash.

It was a bold decision, and a controversial one.

› The Tenacity of Larry Baillie

. . . .

O N MAY 29, 1990, Larry Baillie was driving without a seat belt when a policeman pulled him over. He managed to slip the belt on before the policeman got to his car window, and he congratulated himself on successfully avoiding a ticket.

At the time, Baillie was—wait for this—a stuffed-animal salesman. A native of Scarborough, Ontario, he had joined the armed forces as a youth and been posted to a profoundly boring job at a remote radar station in Saskatchewan. To relieve his boredom at the radar station, he had taken up oil painting, under the tutelage of the padre. Eventually he had been chosen for an exhibition at the Calgary Stampede as one of western Canada's top ten up-and-coming artists. Leaving the military, he worked as an ad salesman for the *Calgary Sun* and the *Winnipeg Sun,* sold photocopiers and then took on a line of stuffed animals. He married and had a son. Life was good.

On May 30, 1990—the day after he had avoided the ticket— Larry Baillie was again driving without a seat belt, buzzing along the highway near Shaunavon, Saskatchewan. A pickup truck ran a stop sign and suddenly appeared in front of Larry's car. Larry hit the pickup at one hundred kilometres per hour. Flying out of his seat, he smashed his head into the windshield.

The resulting brain injury left him totally disabled. He couldn't stand, couldn't walk, couldn't control his emotions. He was forgetful, unable to concentrate and in constant pain. When he tried to walk, he tore his ankle ligaments three times in four weeks. The assessors from Canada Pension Plan (CPP) adjudged him "a-vocational"—unable ever to work or study again. In effect, the system had given up on him, concluding that he would moulder away on a disability pension for the rest of his life.

Larry Baillie disagreed.

"I made myself two promises," Larry remembers. "One, when I learned how to walk I would run a marathon. Two, I was going to go back to school and get back to work again."

A doctor recommended that he learn everything he could about his injury and become an expert on what was happening to his brain and his body. He soon learned that rehabilitation from brain injuries is more successful the earlier it begins, and that the major gains are made within two years of the injury. He concluded that "if I wanted rehabilitation I would have to do it on my own, because the health system was too slow to make the best use of my time. I put together my own program and followed it. It was the hardest task I had ever taken on."

He joined the YMCA and started swimming, eventually extending his time in the pool to ninety minutes a day. He weighed three hundred pounds when he started and worked his way down to 170. He did stretching and exercise. He slowly regained his sense of balance. To develop his hand-eye coordination and exercise his heart, he started playing short-court, a game "similar to squash except it hurts less when you get hit." He also took up bowling.

Three years after his injury, wearing air casts on his legs, he ran a half-marathon. A year later, he ran a full marathon. He has since run eight more. On a wilderness canoe trip, he felt inspired to try his hand at painting once again, this time in watercolours. In 1997, one of his paintings was chosen for a March of Dimes card, and more than a million copies were distributed across the country. His parents, who didn't know he was painting again, received a copy at their home. His mother phoned him in tears.

Baillie's disability didn't go away, but he learned to work with it. He became a Scout leader and a mascot, performing in costume as the Pillsbury Doughboy, the Energizer Bunny and Wesley Coyote, the mascot of the University of Winnipeg sports teams. (Because his pension didn't allow him to earn money, he kept "forgetting" to turn in his pay slips for these jobs.) He visited hospitals as a clown called Dr. Bubbles, a forgetful physician—a persona that turned a weakness into a strength. He learned to do magic stunts, transforming bits of rope into coloured handkerchiefs and using humour to fill in the gaps when he momentarily forgot what he was doing.

"Face it, pace it and get on with it," Larry says. "That's my motto. I still fall, I still have challenges, but it's all about the management of my disability." He continues to struggle with memory, speech, concentration and balance, particularly when he's tired. Because his injury isn't visible, people sometimes assume that he isn't disabled, or that he's dim-witted. He was once thrown off a bus because the driver insisted that he was drunk.

In 2003, having become a passionate advocate for the disabled and marginalized, and frustrated that potential employers "saw my disability before they saw the person," Larry enrolled

24

in Red River College in Winnipeg, earning A+ grades. Two years later, he entered the Bachelor of Social Work program at the University of Manitoba over the strong objections of some administrators and faculty who felt he didn't belong there despite his excellent grades. Then, in 2007, stung by a fellow student's accusation that he'd gotten into university "through the back door," he applied for two national merit-based scholarships. He was particularly interested in the Canada Millennium Scholarships.

"One of the reasons why I was really excited about Millennium was that they had three levels of awards," he recalls, "and I thought maybe I could qualify for the lowest one." Instead, he won the top one, a National In-course Excellence Award. He was stunned. It was as thrilling, he says, as "winning a lottery"—but not because of the money, which was actually a bit less than the bursary he had previously held.

"It was the *recognition* that mattered," Larry explains. "The recognition that it was based on merit and leadership. It was one of the first times in my life that I've been seen for my ability, and not my disability."

In 2008, Larry Baillie graduated from university. He stood at the side of the stage and cried. He found a job as a social worker—and then informed the Canada Pension Plan that he wanted to be taken off their rolls because he wouldn't need their support any more. It was the first such request that the CPP officials had ever encountered.

"I sometimes tell people that my brain injury knocked some sense into my head," Larry jokes. Well, no. But it did provide Larry Baillie with the opportunity to become a brilliant example of courage, determination and intelligence—and not just for the disabled, but for all of us.

> *two*

THE FOUNDATION'S FOUNDATIONS

. . . .

"THE AUDITOR General is *plein de merde*," declared the August Personage, dipping his bread in olive oil and balsamic vinegar after vigorously debating gustatory nuances with the waiter in fluent French. Forceful, knowledgeable and flawlessly bilingual, the August Personage has served the Government of Canada for a lifetime at altitudes so rarefied that the air becomes a little thin in his presence.

"Full of *merde*," the August Personage repeated. "The Auditor General says you shouldn't off-load governmental functions into arm's-length foundations. I say, when you have end-of-the-year money available, it is *highly desirable* to put it into a long-run investment through one of these foundations. These are inherently governmental activities and ideally should be done within government. But if you're going to fund them not from government spending on an annual basis but using year-end money, as was done with the Millennium Scholarship Foundation, that's *exactly* the way to do it. In that situation, a foundation is a very useful vehicle."

The Auditor General registered those complaints in 1999. A decade later, the August Personage was still fuming. The Auditor General had been dismayed by two things. First, the cluster of foundations established by the Chrétien government—mainly aimed at education, research and the creation of a competitive knowledge economy—had been placed beyond the reach of ministerial supervision and parliamentary scrutiny. In the Auditor General's view, they were thus effectively unaccountable for their use of public funds. Second, by shuffling off large amounts of year-end money into the hands of foundations that would spend it over a period of years, the federal government was using foundations as a way to "hide surpluses," thus falsifying the government's accounts. A decade later, in an era of record deficits, that concern sounds quaint.

"The Auditor General's basic critique is that Parliament is voting money that it has no control over," snapped the August Personage. "Well, Parliament is voting with its eyes wide open. Parliament is actually setting up and funding a complete organization, fully elaborated, with an audit function and everything. Parliament has decided that this is desirable.

"The Auditor General would argue that the money should go to pay down the debt instead. Well, sure, it's a good thing to pay down the debt—but that's a political choice. And the politicians decided that this was better, to spend the money on an investment in human capital. Who the hell is the Auditor General to say that they're wrong?

"I believe in the supremacy of Parliament, not the supremacy of the auditors."

An independent organization such as a foundation is indeed beyond the reach of ministerial whims—and that's one of its merits, keeping the organization insulated from short-term political pressures. By the same token, giving the Canada Millennium Scholarship Foundation a ten-year mandate and a sufficient endowment exempted it from the annual scramble for a budget, giving its partners an assurance that they could plan and partner with the organization with the knowledge that it would actually exist, with its funding, for a decade. It wouldn't be dismantled if the government changed. In an environment dominated by short-term politics, the Foundation would be positioned to take a longer view of the public interest within its sphere of operations. One might argue that government could do with more of this, not less.

The Foundation actually had an elaborate accountability structure, largely mandated by the legislation that created it. To begin with, it would be governed by a fifteen-member Board of Directors who were responsible to a group of fifteen "members." After an extensive consultation across the country, the government appointed the first six members, who then appointed nine more. Those fifteen members then appointed nine directors, and the government appointed the remaining six. The appointees were chosen to represent business, public service, education and the student population.

The members appointed the Foundation's auditor, who reported to them. The Board of Directors also had its own audit committee as well as an internal auditor whose reports were available to the external auditor. Every year, the Foundation produced a very extensive annual report, covering its activities, plans and evaluations along with its finances. It circulated the report to the pertinent federal and provincial ministers, distributed it to MPs and Senators, tabled it in both Houses of Parliament and mailed it out to thousands of interested parties across the country. In addition, the annual report was discussed at an annual public meeting held in conjunction with a Foundation-sponsored conference of student financial aid administrators. Foundation officials also appeared before the caucuses of all the political parties in Parliament and before various house committees.

Five years out, Norman Riddell told a government committee that the Foundation's current and past members and directors included three former provincial premiers, two former provincial education ministers, three college presidents, eight former or current university presidents, the heads of the organizations that represented Canada's colleges and universities, six students, nine corporate leaders, three teachers, two representatives of the non-profit sector and the Grand Chief of the Assembly of First Nations. Among the corporations represented were BCE, Alcan, Bombardier, Motorola Canada, Syncrude and Royal Bank.

All of which appears to provide a reasonable degree of accountability. And by 2007, the Auditor General was much happier. The Foundation, said her report, "collects adequate information to report its achievements against objectives, and it meets its obligation to report the results of its activities to Parliament." In the austere language of auditing, this verges on euphoric enthusiasm.

THE ACTUAL creation of the Foundation fell to Human Resources Development Canada. The deputy minister, Mel Cappe, assigned the file to Robert Bourgeois, who is now a vice-president of Laurentian University.

"The legislation had been drafted, but not enacted," Bourgeois says. The Foundation's first chairman had been appointed—Yves

Landry, CEO of Chrysler Canada—but Landry died soon after his appointment, leaving Bourgeois to put together a working group of four or five people in Ottawa and begin the arduous process of selecting members and directors for the Foundation.

"We wanted to ensure that it would have buy-in across the country," Bourgeois explains, citing the need for balance in terms of region, language, gender, ethnicity and the like. "So we had huge banks of potential nominees, which we kept trying to massage until the Privy Council Office felt that they had the right group of individuals that would be generally accepted nationally."

By then, Bourgeois was working with a new chairman of the board—the formidable Jean Monty, CEO of BCE Inc. (formerly Bell Canada Enterprises), a towering figure in Canadian business, who took the job at the personal request of Prime Minister Jean Chrétien. Monty and Bourgeois then drew in Dr. David Smith, former principal of Queen's University, to confer with an array of stakeholders across the country and make recommendations about such matters as the appropriate balance between access bursaries and merit scholarships, issues of eligibility and the definitions of need and merit. Smith presented his report in December 1998. His consultations had revealed an overwhelming consensus that 95 per cent of the awards must be based on financial need. The report also identified a number of options for the Foundation to choose from concerning the determination of need, the distribution of needs-based awards among regions, the average amounts of those awards and the criteria for awarding and administering the 5 per cent of the funds that would be devoted to merit scholarships.

The Foundation was incorporated in June 1998 and issued a call for tenders to manage its money. In July 1998, its endowment—$2.5 billion—was transferred to the new organization. Even that was tricky, says Robert Bourgeois, because moving such huge sums into the market can actually create a bubble of apparent demand that will influence the prices of the securities involved, "so it had to be done in stages, in ways that didn't distort the market.

"We had some interesting debates—some good honest arguments with Mel Cappe and Jean Monty talking about whether the awards should be skewed towards practical programs, like engineering and commerce, and so on. I remember Mel arguing very forcefully that society needs poets and philosophers, and that we should not be forgetting that education is about more than just science and engineering. In the end he prevailed. I think that was a good decision. Another good decision was that the awards should be mostly devoted to access.

"Monty was a fun guy to work with," Bourgeois says, "and he brought a lot to the process. He used his communication director in BCE to come up with the Foundation's logo and its look and all that. I'll never forget the day when we were sitting in his boardroom, and he brought these folks in with the mock-ups and so on, and they set them up at the end of the boardroom table. This is the kind of meeting that, if it were in government, the process would go on for weeks if not months. But Jean looked at this stuff and said, 'Yeah, that looks fine to me, what do you guys think? Let's vote. Decided!' It was done in about five minutes."

It was largely through Monty's influence that the Foundation established its offices in Montreal.

"That was a strategic choice," nods the August Personage. "If you'd put it in Ottawa, there would have been a question about whether it was really arm's-length. Furthermore, it was obvious that the Foundation would have to build a bridge to Quebec—and Montreal is the headquarters of Quebec, so to speak, but not the capital. So you're in neither a federal nor a provincial capital, and you can talk to all capitals. By the same token, the Foundation had four francophone chairs. Not an accident. Symbolism counts."

"Jean Monty was absolutely the right person to get us going," says John Stubbs, the former president of Simon Fraser University and a board member throughout the entire life of the Foundation. "His appointment was a stroke of genius, primarily because of his ability to pick up the phone and talk with any premier in the country and say, 'Look, you've got to get onside here.' I would love to have been a silent observer of that process." He laughs. "I never saw anyone run a meeting like Monty. Bang, bang, bang. No repetition allowed. Sorry, he'd say, that point has already been made. Next?"

Communications director Jean Lapierre has a similar memory. He was scheduled to present his communications strategy to the board, and when the time came, "there was ten minutes left before twelve o'clock, and M. Monty didn't want to be there after lunch. He said to me, 'Can you present your communications plan in ten minutes? If you can't, you're fired.'"

Monty may not have been joking. Alex Usher was the Foundation's top policy officer at the time, and he remembers that Monty's philosophy was that "the job of the board is to agree with the staff. If the level of agreement drops below 99 per cent, we get a new staff."

As a federal agency, even at arm's length, the new Foundation wasn't entirely welcome in Quebec. In fact, it even had difficulty finding office space to rent. So Monty also provided the Foundation with its first offices—"a closet in Monty's building" says Usher—and then had to explain to the other tenants in the building why the entrance to their building was, at one point, being blocked by student protesters.

"You can imagine our first couple of meetings," says Jeannie Lea, the former PEI Minister of Advanced Education who served on the Board of Directors from the outset. "We have this superstar CEO chairing it, and we always met in the Bell building either in Montreal or Toronto. Monty was a no-nonsense guy, and you could see how he operated as a CEO. In fact the members of the board never really got to know each other then, because Monty didn't have time for small talk and socializing. A fascinating man."

AMONG THE most important decisions the board ever made was appointing Norman Riddell as executive director and chief executive officer, effective January 25, 1999.

"That appointment was very controversial, for a couple of reasons," said the August Personage. "First, he was an anglophone, and how are you going to get cooperation from Quebec if he's an anglophone? Second, he had been a Quebec public servant, so how are you going to keep this national if you base it in Montreal and put it in the hands of a former Quebec public servant? So he was damned for being an anglophone and also for being a Quebecker. Remarkable. But I thought that if he bought the Foundation any credibility with Quebec at all, it was going to be worthwhile, because it was clear that that was going to be the most critical negotiation—and even if they hated him in Quebec, they would at least answer his phone calls.

"Also, a lot of people didn't think he had a national perspective. So I was told it was a bad appointment."

Wait a minute. This is a man from Moose Jaw, Saskatchewan, who earned a Ph.D. from Stanford University in California with a thesis on the teleological tradition in English political thought. His professional career began in the Department of Foreign

34

Affairs in Ottawa and overseas. He later became a cabinet secretary in Saskatchewan, where he was deeply involved in the
Meech Lake federal–provincial negotiations on the constitution
of Canada. Then he became the Quebec deputy minister responsible for immigration, working very comfortably in French—and
in that capacity he negotiated and implemented what he consid-
ers to be "the only part of Meech that actually happened, namely
the transfer of authority over immigration to Quebec." He later
moved to Edmonton as associate vice-president of the University
of Alberta.

No national perspective?

"Well, yeah, they were wrong," said the August Personage.
"And he had a vision of what the Foundation could be. I've been
impressed by what he accomplished."

Norman Riddell did indeed have a vision of a new type of
public-sector organization. He was fifty-five, and the Foundation
was potentially the cap of his career. He agreed with then–
Finance Minister Paul Martin that foundations—"para-public
organizations," as one commentator described them—could provide a new and more effective way of doing some kinds of public
business. His new appointment provided him with a glorious
opportunity to show just how effectively public business could
and should be conducted.

Within government, he later reflected, "I had managed
organizations that were very structured, with a great deal of
emphasis on process. I had an idea of another kind of organization, but I didn't know really what it would be like to be in
one. Well, we created it and discovered what it was like, and how
you'd have to manage in this environment. It isn't the same as
being a deputy minister and managing a department with fifteen hundred people in it. It's just completely different."

In truth, Riddell had become quite disillusioned about normal routines of government, though not, he hastens to say, "about the role of government to do good in society. But I became really concerned that government as we know it now is putting an inordinate amount of importance on process and not nearly enough on results. So you get people saying, 'Well, I followed all the rules. It doesn't really matter whether the clients are changed or not.' In fact you don't even ask the question. But you've always got to answer that question: did the client get something?

"So we would build an organization where process was cut down to the minimum," he continued. "We would also build an organization that was as small as possible, because I had found that as you added more people, you needed more process to manage their relations. So I said at the outset that we're not going to have an HR department, we're not going to have a legal department, we're not going to have an IT department. We're going to have all this stuff outside. We're only going to do the stuff that only we can do. We're going to work in partnership with people, and our job is to hook all the pieces together. And because our organization was small, the individuals in it had to be of a certain kind and they had to be managed in a certain way. This couldn't be a terribly hierarchical organization. You had to give people broad mandates and then let them fill them in themselves."

36

Ultimately, the Foundation would consist of about forty people, all on a single floor of a Montreal office building, and the efficiency of its lean structure is neatly captured in a comment by Andrew Parkin, the Foundation's last associate executive director.

"I remember we were meeting with the Auditor General's group when we were audited in '07," Parkin says. "And they were asking us about the collection of information on complaints from students. What was the process? And I said, 'Well, people call the switchboard, and Maria, who's our information officer who runs the reception, passes them on to whoever should talk to them about a particular problem. And if there is something that went wrong, so let's say there was a mistake in a form letter and it causes a spike in the number of calls, Maria will know. I mean she'll just know that she keeps getting all these calls from students from New Brunswick and that's unusual so she'll know.'

"So the next thing was they said, 'Okay, then presumably then these are all logged in.' 'Well, yes, Maria takes notes of calls.' And they said, 'So do you get a monthly report and then at the end of every month do you have a meeting about the monthly report?' And I said, 'No, you missed something. If Maria's getting a lot of calls from New Brunswick, she'll tell Norman—because Norman walks past her desk a hundred times a day. And Norman will come find one of us and get us to fix it as soon as we can. And there's no memo, and there's no meeting.'"

The Foundation would also reward employee successes in the most tangible way. A substantial part of every employee's pay would be conditional, and "the higher you go, the more your pay is at risk," says Riddell. "I'll tell you to expect to make, say, $60,000 a year—but I'm only going to pay you $45,000 of it during the year, and you get the other $15,000 if you meet all of your objectives. So your bonus is much bigger, but it's contingent on results. What did you deliver for the organization? You deliver, you get; you don't, you don't. It's very clear, and by and large people have stepped up to the plate, used their creativity and delivered more than we asked them to do. But that's the kind of thing that makes this a really different kind of place.

"Another thing was that we were going to be ready to admit

mistakes. I firmly believe that I make at least one mistake a day, and it seems to be totally silly to do what we do in the Westminster system, which is to say that everybody who sits on the Speaker's right is always 100 per cent right, and those who sit on the Speaker's left are always 100 per cent wrong. That's just silly and stupid."

And right at the core of the organizational plan stood a single figure: the Canadian student, the person for whom the whole apparatus had been constructed.

"This comes from Jean Monty," says Riddell, "but it's an attitude I shared with him and with the board. We were given two and a half billion dollars. It's rather a lot of money, and we really believed that we should use it for the people it was voted for. So that's partly the reason why the organization was small, because everything you burned up in administration was something you didn't give to young people, or use to find out something that would help in designing programs to serve them better. It was an ethical question. You used the money for the clients. That is what it was voted for."

The result was a curious attitude to money, which might be described as parsimony without fussiness. If there's a need to spend money to serve the mission, you don't fuss about it; you spend what you need to spend. For instance, the Foundation believed strongly in evaluation—because how else do you know if you're getting results?—and was perfectly willing to spend money on rigorous evaluations. On the other hand, it relied very heavily on cooperative ventures—with the provinces in particular, but also with organizations like the World Petroleum Council (WPC) and the YMCA—and it made extensive use of volunteers both within its programs and in such roles as conference speakers. Board members were entitled to a modest stipend, but many, including Monty, never collected it.

The overarching theme of the Foundation, says Riddell, was change. "It was about positive change, about growth. Whether it was the employees who worked at the Foundation, or the clients that we were supposed to be developing, or the people that we were hoping would eventually become our clients, it was always about changing people in a positive direction."

An institution, wrote Ralph Waldo Emerson, is "the lengthened shadow of a man." In the case of the Canada Millennium Scholarship Foundation, that man was Norman Riddell, which is quite remarkable, given that he reported to a very strong board and surrounded himself with very strong colleagues. Medium height, balding and bespectacled, generally wearing a navy suit with white shirt and correct tie, he looks the embodiment of a cautious bureaucrat. He is not. He has an entrepreneur's cool acceptance of risk, an athlete's focus on measurable results and an evangelist's passion for provoking transformation.

He is a shy but passionate man. He loves music and seriously considered a career as a concert pianist. He still plays, says a colleague, "magnificently." He also loves model trains. When he was a young diplomat in Senegal, he fell in love with a woman on sight; they were married in five months, and they are still married. An old friend describes Claudia Riddell as a strong and determined person, and the relationship as "very lively—but he is utterly devoted to her." Riddell has a list of places he wants to see before he dies, and he is methodically checking them off. When he's seized by a beguiling new idea, he tends to forget that his people are already fully loaded, and if one balks at signing on for the additional work, he can be "aggressively unsympathetic." In his pursuit of a flat, small organization, he "brutally understaffed the Foundation initially," says one old hand, with the result that his people were constantly balancing on the lip of burn-out.

Voices in the air. Voices in the corridors.

Norman is incredibly bright, and he has intense curiosity. He's very good at getting what he wants.

He's very demanding. A perfectionist. He's been called a slave driver. Not by me.

He's perfectly capable of dressing you down in public, and that's not a pleasant experience.

There's a values thing that comes from the top and it's strong and it's clear and it's a testament to Norman. He is unfailing in the values piece.

He's a force of nature and a fantastic boss as long as you can keep him moving forward. If he starts to look inward, that's bad news.

As old-fashioned as he is, he is by far the most open boss I've ever had, and the least micro managing. But if you don't have his trust, he'll micro manage you to death.

He's a very good negotiator—and sometimes people don't even know they've been negotiated.

His unswerving focus on the mandate and the responsibility to use the money well has been crucial.

His leadership has been transformative.

So it's January 1999, and you're Norman Riddell, and you're in charge of Canada's largest millennium project, and the Prime Minister wants cheques going out to students in the first days of the new millennium. That gives you eleven months to put the whole apparatus in place—finance and administration, bursary program, excellence awards, communication and promotion, everything. Go!

You need people. You're charged with handing out at least 100,000 bursaries every year, and, eventually, nine hundred excellence scholarships as well. For starters, you'll need accountants, database and systems administrators, a receptionist. The Excellence Award Program will require people to define excellence and create an application process, which means that you're going to need a communications staff and an awards staff to administer the process and then another group of people—a large group—to adjudicate the applications.

On the bursary side, you're going to need staff to identify students in need and get the bursaries out to them. Since the legislation directs you to work cooperatively with the provinces and avoid duplication, you're going to have to negotiate a whole series of agreements with the provinces—immediately. You're facing a tornado of protest from the provinces, who feel that the government that created the Foundation created its surplus by off-loading many of its obligations onto them. Someone has to soothe and seduce those prickly provinces.

"I think that most people that might have been hired for Norman's job would not have been able to do what he managed to do," says Andrew Woodall, the director of the Millennium Excellence Awards Program, who joined the Foundation in midstream. "And that's partly because of the people he hired early on." The Foundation hired four senior people in fairly short order: Paul Bourque, chief financial officer; Jean Lapierre, director of communications; Alex Usher, senior policy officer; and Franca Gucciardi, national coordinator of the Excellence Awards Program.

Franca Gucciardi was twenty-eight and had just resigned as associate director at the Canadian Merit Scholarship Foundation in Toronto, which awards a small number of large and prestigious scholarships annually. She was planning to study for a Ph.D., but then she got a call from Norman Riddell.

"He asked me if I would be interested in helping to set up a merit program," she remembers. "I said no, and he said, 'Look, before you decide, why don't you come and see me for a weekend in Montreal?' A weekend in Montreal? Hmm . . . okay. So I went to see him, believing that this would just be a bureaucratic exercise.

"When I met with Norman, I actually wanted him to give me reasons to turn it down. I asked all kinds of questions—who gets to decide on the criteria, who gets to decide on the selection process and so on—and it became really clear that he was actually asking for me to come and do it, that he really wanted my very particular vision about merit scholarships.

"So then I said yes—and two weeks later I found myself in Montreal in front of a computer, saying, 'Okay, let's design this program.' Within six months, we had the design of the process approved by the board, we had written the application, I had recruited all the assessors and we had done our first selection process.

"It was pretty incredible to be part of this team with Alex and Norman—which in many ways was a triad—and to have such a huge budget, such an opportunity to do something really big. It was really inspiring every day to go to work. There was an energy in the air that I would never have associated with government funding. I mean, I literally turned on my computer and wrote the program, and who would have possibly imagined that you could do that? And then you'd have conversations with your peers that would just keep getting better based on what everybody would contribute. It was magic in those first few years when we were creating the whole thing."

Voices in the air. Voices in the corridors.

Franca did an amazing job. Wonderful.

Everything is controlled, crisp, all the processes written down.

The selection process Franca created is brilliant.
Franca would have made an absolutely superb general.

Alex Usher had been a student leader and in 1995 had led a contingent of member schools out of the Canadian Federation of Students (CFS) to form the Canadian Alliance of Student Associations (CASA). For the CFS, Norman Riddell later reflected ruefully, hiring Usher was "like hiring the devil, and we never got over that." As late as 2007, the CFS was still excoriating the Foundation as "a failed experiment in student financial aid, a public relations gimmick" administering "a provincial patchwork of programs that struggle to be classified as financial aid."

Usher is brilliant, mercurial, impatient and droll. After graduating from McGill, he had gone to work for the Association of Universities and Colleges of Canada. There he had been heavily involved in drafting the student assistance reform initiative presented to the government by the Roundtable on Student Assistance, which included all the national groups representing students, faculty, universities and colleges. The roundtable was advocating a whole package of measures, including provisions for educational savings plans, withdrawals from RRSPs for educational purposes, more flexibility in student loans—and a national granting program.

Usher subsequently became part of the lobbying effort—and the effort was successful. The educational content of the 1998 federal budget was "all about us," he says. "We got everything. It wasn't quite the way we'd asked for it—a foundation hadn't been on our agenda—but the basic push in terms of grants and improvements to loans and creation of educational savings programs and all those kinds of things, we'd done it."

In doing the research for the roundtable's submissions, Usher had closely examined student aid not only across Canada, but also in the United States and elsewhere. As a result, he had a broad understanding of student aid at the national level, an expertise that made him almost unique. He was not altogether surprised when Norman Riddell called him and asked if he'd be interested in helping him to negotiate with the provinces. He became senior policy officer and later took on the job of creating the Foundation's trail-blazing research program.

Voices in the air:

Alex is almost a myth around here, or a legend, and sometimes a caricature.

He has a keen intellect, and a sharp eye for where things are heading.

Alex doesn't suffer fools lightly.

He's a huge soccer fan, and he's good company. He's funny and engaging.

Alex Usher is a cocky bastard, not someone I particularly like— but boy! He did a great job for the Foundation.

He's had a very significant impact on the landscape of the world in which we work, student financial aid, and, indeed, post-secondary education in Canada.

THE FOUNDATION that emerged from the frenzied activity of 1999 was, at its very core, an organization that loved education, loved young people, enjoyed their company and enjoyed watching them grow.

One of the Foundation's conferences for Excellence Award winners involved a treasure hunt in downtown Ottawa, and in the course of the chase, Norman Riddell found himself trapped in an elevator with about fifteen of the students.

"We're packed in," says Riddell. "We're stuck in the elevator for quite a long time. But these kids could organize themselves at a drop of a hat . . . boom. So they organize it that everybody's going to tell something interesting about themselves. They're from all over Canada; they haven't had really a chance to meet each other very much. They see this as an opportunity to get to know about each other.

"One young man says that what's been really important to him is that in the past year he's become the assistant pastor at his church. Well, a lot of what motivates people in community service is faith-based, and it has to be respected. It isn't always as well respected by secular urban societies as it might be. And back in the corner behind me is a young girl from Toronto who says, 'Well, I had a great summer job. I reviewed porn.'

"Do you know what the guy who was the assistant pastor says to that? He says, 'What makes good porn?' Completely honest question. His attitude was just, 'Okay that's what you do, I'm not judging you, but would you please help me understand what's going on here?' Now, I'm familiar with people like him in western Canada, and they usually regard pornography as just morally depraved. But he wasn't treating her as though she was morally depraved at all.

"That's what that program did, I think. It didn't tell anybody that you should be a fundamentalist or that you should be a reviewer of porn; it didn't tell them that at all. It promoted an idea about education: be inquiring, suspend judgement, look for facts, have respect, keep the emotions out of the argument and see where it takes you. And that's what an education is really about."

45

> A Dynasty of Scholars

. . . .

"A FTER THE three of us got the scholarships, I think Mom and Dad adored going out to parties and that type of thing," says Erin Aylward, "because they were always being asked, 'So what did you guys do?'"

Good question. Geoff and Elaine Aylward live in Mount Pearl, Newfoundland, a suburb of St. John's. All three of their children—Stephen, twenty-one; Erin, twenty; and Meaghan, nineteen—have won Millennium Excellence Awards. They are not the only family to capture multiple awards. At least eight other families have won two or more Excellence Awards, and a couple of families have won three.

So what accounts for such success? What did the Aylward family do right?

"We've been really, really blessed in our parents and our grandparents—our dad's father and mother, who live in St. John's," says Erin. "Speaking for myself, I've been surrounded by unconditional love and support my whole life, and it's been a major factor in my gaining confidence and taking initiatives."

And, says Erin, the Aylwards were really fortunate in having gone to Holy Heart of Mary High School, "which is so tolerant, and has such a thriving community of music and sports and art. The school has so much potential for leadership, and the staff has always been so supportive of the initiatives that students have taken on."

Meaghan agrees—and adds a further ingredient.

"Within the three of us there was always a lot of support for all of our different projects," she says. "If Stephen was having a bottle drive, for instance, then Erin and I would both go. We would always help each other out that way."

Erin and Meaghan both live at home and attend Memorial University. Stephen is at McGill University in Montreal. All three did French immersion and completed the demanding international baccalaureate (IB) program at Holy Heart.

With one thousand students, Holy Heart is the province's largest high school and the only one that offers the IB program. It is also one of the few Newfoundland schools that offer English as a second language, which gives it an unusually diverse and cosmopolitan student body. Holy Heart is a power in hockey and rugby—Erin is a rugby player—and participates strongly in academic competitions like Shad Valley and the Canada Wide Science Fair. Its chamber choir won an international gold medal in Vienna some years ago and regularly competes and tours overseas.

All three Aylwards also sang in Shallaway, the internationally celebrated youth chorus of Newfoundland, which tours internationally every year—most recently to Argentina, France, Spain, Denmark, the U.S. and Ireland.

Holy Heart must be one of the few high schools in Canada to have a long-standing social justice committee, which all three

Aylwards chaired in their senior years. The school's Interact organization—a youth branch of Rotary—has partnered with Syed Pasha school in Kandahar, Afghanistan, and recently raised $1,500 to buy books, school supplies and playground equipment. The school's own Amnesty group meets every Wednesday at noon, and Steve Aylward was a major player in that group, too. The idea came from his grandfather, a retired judge.

"I remember watching the evening news one time with my grandfather, and I was just horrified by a shot of some tanks rolling into a city somewhere. I asked my grandfather, 'Is there anything that can be done to prevent all the suffering in the world?' It was a very idealistic moment for a thirteen- or fourteen-year-old. And he suggested that I look into Amnesty International.

"So I became quite involved with Amnesty International in St. John's, and then later here in Montreal and in Germany, in Freiburg, where I was on exchange last year. I went to Mexico in 2007 as a youth delegate for Amnesty International Canada, and I'm going to Ottawa pretty soon for a meeting of the international strategy committee."

The thirst for social justice has led Meaghan into working with Oxfam and with a non-profit called the Mercy Centre for Ecology and Justice. She's headed a fundraising initiative to raise money to provide educational opportunity for girls in Kenya, and she also works with the World Health Organization in its drive to eradicate polio—an effort headed by her uncle, who operates out of Switzerland. Erin, meanwhile, took a course in Spanish at Holy Heart, fell in love with the language, visited Argentina, Ecuador and Nicaragua, serves as regional youth liaison for Oxfam Canada and is deeply involved with a campaign to inject more awareness of global issues into the province's school system.

Geoff and Elaine Aylward clearly did do some things very right. So what did they actually do?

Two things, say their children. First, unconditional love. Second, the Aylwards always expressed a sense that post-secondary education was "a stepping stone to all kinds of opportunities," as Elaine puts it. The Aylwards had been saving money in Registered Educational Savings Plans for each of the children, and as they approached the end of high school, Elaine had spent a lot of time researching scholarships.

"Our mom had an account with every single scholarship search engine online," Meaghan laughs. "And we would be working on something in our room, and she would find an application and come in and say, 'That's due in two weeks! Get your transcript.'

"I think that's part of that unconditional support, because looking for scholarships online is really daunting, and even when I looked at the Millennium application, I thought, 'Uhh, I don't know if I'm cut out for this.' And having Mom there to say, 'Nope, you are. No harm in trying'—having that kind of extra support was a huge factor for us."

Elaine is also amused at the memory, but as early as Grade 9 she was pointing Stephen towards the Millennium awards.

"I just felt that Millennium had so many opportunities, like all of the networking and the friendships and the leadership opportunities, certainly an excellent program," she says. And she was already looking farther ahead—"not just the undergrad degree, but what comes beyond in terms of a master's or doctoral program. I was trying to line up as many resources as possible to fund not just the undergrad program, but whatever might lie beyond that."

And now Stephen is just finishing his degree in philosophy and political science. (Erin is doing political science and Spanish,

Meaghan political science and psychology.) Stephen says, "I've barricaded myself in my room," working on his graduating thesis. What comes next for him?

"I'm going to Oxford next year," he says. "I was selected as the Rhodes Scholar for Newfoundland for 2008–09, and I'm going to study law at St. Hilda's College."

Why are we not surprised? And no doubt your sisters will follow in due course.

> *three*

AN ESSAY UPON ELEPHANTS

. . . .

WITH ITS core staff in place, the Foundation embarked on a whirlwind of creation and invention that Alex Usher describes as "three years of almost constant innovation." By all accounts, it was like managing a stampede of mustangs.

"My favourite week was the first week of May 1999," he remembers, chuckling. "We left Sunday night to go to Toronto. We signed a deal in Toronto on the Monday and [we were] in Alberta on the Tuesday, and then Wednesday I had a half day at home in Ottawa. Then we flew out to Newfoundland for a first meeting with the deputy minister on Thursday. On Thursday afternoon we're flying out for a ceremony in Manitoba Friday morning, and I get a call from Brady Salloum in Saskatchewan saying that the premier wants to sign Friday afternoon.

"And I said, 'Wait, Brady. One, we haven't decided on about 90 per cent of the content of this thing, and two, there's no commercial flight that gets us to Saskatoon by that time.' And

Brady said, 'That's okay, the premier will send his plane to Winnipeg to pick you up.' Well, I'm actually from Winnipeg, and I was at home sitting at my parents' kitchen table talking on the phone with Brady and his deputy minister, and literally we got the details of the Saskatchewan deal done between his kitchen table and mine that night. Next day the premier's plane picked us up and we flew to Saskatoon and signed the deal, and then we flew home.

"I just burst into giggles on the plane home because we'd given away over a billion dollars and flown about ten thousand miles—in one week. And we didn't even have our own offices yet. In fact, I wasn't even an employee yet. I was working on contract for the first three months I was there."

That was May. British Columbia, Nova Scotia and the Yukon signed in June. The Northwest Territories and Prince Edward Island signed in July, while Nunavut, New Brunswick and Newfoundland followed in August. The last agreement was with Quebec, always wary of federal initiatives.

Quebec is uniquely sensitive to intrusions into its jurisdiction in education—and properly so, given the importance of education to the health of the French language and culture. But all the provinces share such sensitivities to greater or lesser degrees, and every province is different. As a result, federal–provincial jousting is arguably Canada's second-favourite sport, after hockey. There is a very Canadian story about four people being asked to write an essay on the subject of elephants. The Englishman writes on "The Significance of the Elephant in Ceremonial Processions in India." The German expounds on "Military Uses of the Elephant." The French writer chooses "The Love Life of the Elephant." The Canadian's paper is entitled "The Elephant: Is He a Federal or a Provincial Responsibility?"

The Foundation's various provincial agreements had two things in common. First, the amount of money committed to each province was in proportion to that province's share of the Canadian population. Second, the money had to go directly to the support of needy students—but the arrangements for doing that were shaped by the individual province's needs and wishes. The result was a vivid example of "asymmetrical federalism," where the provinces are treated individually within an equitable overall framework. And though the Quebec agreement was the last to be signed, the need to accommodate Quebec had shaped the Foundation's whole approach to the provinces right from the start.

In 1998, when the Foundation was created, the Quebec National Assembly had passed a resolution laying down the guidelines it expected the Millennium scholarships to follow. Sponsored by a Member of the National Assembly named Henri-François Gautrin, the resolution had three requirements. First, the amount of money to be spent in Quebec should be proportional to Quebec's population within Canada. Second, Quebec should select the recipients of the scholarships. Third, the scholarships should be advanced to the recipients in a way that avoided all duplication and provided the federal government with "the necessary visibility." The motion also acknowledged the intention of Quebec to dedicate the amounts that it would save from its own scholarship programs to the funding of colleges and universities.

"One of my first tasks was to plan the negotiations," Norman Riddell remembers. "And I had a whole bunch of unfriendly provinces to deal with; Quebec wasn't the only one. Well, we thought about it and we came fairly rapidly to the conclusion that Quebec would be last. Then we looked very carefully at the Gautrin resolution and tried to imagine how we could run our program consistent with its terms. We came up with an idea of how to do that, and we took that idea to Alberta. What we were aiming for was an agreement with Alberta that would meet all the terms of the Gautrin resolution.

"So we went to Alberta and said, 'Look, we have a debt-reduction program here that we can adapt to different provincial realities. What we're interested in is helping Alberta students. You've got 10 per cent of the country's population, so you're entitled to 10 per cent of the funds. That would be $300 million over the next ten years.' And we wound up co-funding and extending an existing program in Alberta—they did the first year, we did the second, third and fourth years."

The Foundation took the same proportional and cooperative approach with all the provinces, and Riddell was delighted with the diversity of the resulting programs.

"If ten different things are done in the ten provinces, then we can compare the results and learn from one another," he says. "The program becomes a whole series of natural experiments. Nova Scotia, for instance, put all its money into first-year scholarships. New Brunswick spread the money over three years—so now we can compare the effectiveness of these two approaches.

"At the Foundation, we think the diversity of Canada is a strength, not a problem. Really, it's a different view of the federation. You collaborate. You work with what's there. We've shown a way for federal agencies to exercise soft leadership while respecting the autonomy of the provinces."

Initially, however, Quebec—then governed by the Parti Québécois—refused to talk to the Foundation at all. It took the position that the government of Quebec negotiates with other governments, not with strange excrescences like foundations— and that the feds should simply turn the money over to Quebec

54

and let Quebec give it to the students. The federal government, however, couldn't do that, even if it wanted to, because the Foundation was essentially an independent body, and the $2.5 billion had already been handed over to it. Ottawa didn't have the money and could not write the cheque itself, nor could it direct the Foundation to do so.

At this juncture, Riddell managed to arrange a meeting with the editor-in-chief of *La Presse,* Quebec's largest French-language newspaper, where he suggested that the editor might like to review the Alberta agreement in the light of the Gautrin resolution. If the Foundation was prepared to respect Gautrin—and had already done so elsewhere—why should Quebec have a problem signing on? The editor agreed and said so in print.

But Quebec still wouldn't talk directly to the Foundation. So the federal government offered to negotiate on its behalf. It sent two officials—one was Robert Bourgeois—to begin a dialogue. The resulting draft agreement involved minor compromises on both sides but was essentially acceptable—with one great omission, the issue of "displacement." The draft did not specify that Foundation money would provide new *and additional* support to the students. This meant that Quebec would have been allowed to reduce its own support for students exactly in proportion to the new support from the Foundation. The Foundation would put $70 million into the hands of students, but the Quebec government would take $70 million away from them, "and no Quebec student would be a dime better off," says Riddell. "Well, the board wondered why we'd be paying $70 million to get nothing for the people that Parliament told us we were supposed to benefit."

Up until this point, the Quebec student movement had been warmly supporting the provincial government against the evil federal Foundation. Now Riddell and his colleagues sat down with student leader Daniel Baril and briefed him on the situation.

"We pointed out to him that if we signed the agreement as it was being proposed, no student would be better off," he says. "And we suggested that it wouldn't look too good if he agreed to a deal where $70 million more goes in, and the only people who benefit are the Government of Quebec."

Baril now took an active interest in the process and ultimately brokered an agreement. Quebec sets a limit on a student's indebtedness, and under the terms of the Baril proposal, the Quebec government agreed to lower those limits by about 25 per cent for ten years, thus reducing the debt of every student in the province. The province also agreed to provide $35 million to Quebec's colleges and universities specifically for improvements in student services and limitations on student ancillary fees—lab fees, library fees, activity fees and the like.

There remained one more Gilbert-and-Sullivan episode as the deal was completed. Although the framework of an agreement was in place, Quebec still wouldn't talk directly to the Foundation. So Robert Bourgeois set up a process of shuttle diplomacy, talking to each participant in turn and gradually finalizing the agreement.

"You know one of the big sticking issues?" says Bourgeois. "The cheques. What was going to be on the cheques that students would receive? Canada wanted to issue Canadian cheques and the Quebec government said, 'No way! We want the fleur-de-lys on it, and we want our logo, and it's got to come through our system.' It was almost hilarious." Indeed, the debate over the cheques spawned a whole flurry of solemn correspondence between François Legault, the Quebec minister, and Pierre Pettigrew and Jane Stewart, the successive federal ministers. (In the end, the logos of both Quebec and the Foundation appeared in the upper corners of the cheques, which were actually printed by the Quebec government.) The discussions ended in "proximity negotiations," with the Quebec negotiators installed in one hotel room, the Foundation officials in another and Robert Bourgeois trotting back and forth between the two.

And so the Quebec deal was done, on December 22, 1999, just in time for the first bursary cheques to be issued on the fourth day of the new millennium, January 4, 2000. The arrangement came unglued briefly in 2005 when the subsequent Liberal government of Quebec attempted to raise the student-loan thresholds again, in contravention of the agreement. Jean Lapierre, the Foundation's director of communications, read about the proposals in the newspapers, called Norman Riddell, conferred with a Quebec ministerial staffer about the implications and proposed a strategy to Riddell. Riddell then wrote privately to the minister, which ruffled some feathers, given that Quebec still did not officially recognize the Foundation's existence. In his letter, Riddell pointed out that the change would deprive the students of the benefits that had been negotiated, thus rendering the agreement pointless. The Foundation therefore saw no justification for continuing to transfer funds to Quebec. It then turned off the tap.

And then it waited—for thirteen months—while Ottawa fretted and Quebec fumed.

Once again, Quebec's students broke the impasse. When the students realized that their loans were increasing and that the provincial government had disrupted the flow of student aid from the Foundation, they marched in the streets—100,000 of them. Shortly afterwards, the premier shuffled the cabinet. Discreet conversations began between the Foundation and the new minister and deputy. The resulting compromise brought the loan thresholds back down over two years, and the Foundation committed an additional $10 million a year—which was Quebec's share of a new Access Bursary Program anyway. And the money flowed again.

The Quebec agreement—in an area of "contested" jurisdiction—was carefully considered by the formidable former editor of *Le Devoir* and former leader of the Quebec Liberals, Claude Ryan, a Quebec nationalist so authoritative that he was known as "the pope of rue St.-Jacques." Ryan ultimately accepted that the federal government did have a legitimate interest in student aid and concluded that the Foundation's approach provided "an example that we would be wise to emulate in seeking solutions to many other issues that divide us as Canadians, when they should instead be uniting us in the same concern for better serving the people of this country."

JANET ECKER, later a member of the Foundation's board, was Ontario's Minister of Education when the Foundation was created. She vividly remembers the high-handedness of the usual federal approach, and the refreshing novelty of the Foundation's willingness to construct a different deal for every province, so long as the ultimate result in every case was an appropriate improvement in provincial support for needy students.

"Very often, in the federal–provincial sphere, Ottawa would come up with a bright new idea and sort of drop it on everybody's dinner table like a hand grenade," she says. "They wouldn't pay attention to some of the subtleties about how to implement or integrate the new federal initiative with existing provincial programs—and the Chrétien government was actually quite bad about this.

"So the Canada Millennium Scholarship Foundation was a great idea, but the way that the concept was delivered created not only political problems for various provincial governments, but also problems for students or recipients. A lot of anger and irritation was built up not only about the intrusion into what was considered a provincial jurisdiction, but also the way it was done, leaving the provinces to pick up the pieces and deal with it.

"I think it was one of the great accomplishments of the Foundation to figure out how to work with the provinces so that it respected provincial jurisdiction but at the same time made sure that the dollars went to where they were supposed to be going. The Foundation is really one of the great unsung success stories of federal–provincial relations."

A particularly brilliant feature of the Foundation's strategy in these negotiations lay in its acceptance of the second point in the Gautrin resolution—Quebec's insistence that the province should select the recipients of the bursaries, along with the later requirement that Quebec should issue the actual cheques. The federal government's assumption had been that the Foundation would select the bursary recipients itself and would therefore have to create its own huge administrative structure, says Alex Usher, with hundreds of staff that would make it "almost a parallel Canada Student Loans Program. And I think, frankly, there were some people in the Liberal administration who thought that was a really good idea."

The conventional expectation in Ottawa was that the administrative costs would be about 15 per cent of the amount that the program delivered. The Foundation undertook to distribute at least 100,000 scholarships valued at $3,000 every year, for a total of $300 million. A 15 per cent administrative budget would thus amount to about $45 million. But if the Foundation were not going to run its programs separately, and would not insist that its program be exactly the same in every part of the country, then it would have no need of a vast bureaucracy. Instead, it could deliver its bursaries through provincial student aid offices, and its net administrative costs proved to be about 4 per cent.

In addition, Usher says dryly, Riddell looked for savings in every possible cranny, enlisting a vast number of volunteers, keeping the staff small and generally making "a fetish of saving on administration." (Usher, says Riddell, "was probably one of the least polite employees I ever had, and would frequently— well not frequently, but every once in a while—call me an idiot." Most people, says another Foundation employee, "would have fired Alex for the stuff he said, but Norman said, 'I needed him for something that he was good at.'")

In the Foundation's 1999 annual report, Jean Monty summarized the results of the first full year of operations, including the cost benefits of working cooperatively with the provinces. First, said Monty, the Foundation "established and delivered a bursary program that has already provided more than $275 million of badly needed assistance to more than 90,000 young Canadians who are enrolled in private vocational schools, community colleges or universities. Second, it succeeded in convincing 13 provinces and territories to become partners in the administration of its program. As a result, the Foundation has been able to deliver its bursary program at less than one-quarter of the cost originally projected. Over the next 10 years these savings should permit the Foundation to provide an additional 300 million dollars of assistance to needy students."

Those savings would do much more than that. They would also finance a research program that would provide Canadians with a much more profound, complex and useful understanding of the real barriers to higher education, provide enough money for an entire additional bursary program specifically directed at the most needy students in the country, and allow the Foundation to enhance its Excellence Awards with a series of enrichment programs.

The one disappointment in the negotiations, says Robert Bourgeois, was the very issue which had been so difficult in Quebec: the issue of displacement, or "incrementality"—the idea that the Foundation's bursaries should be additional funds for the student and should not simply take the place of funding already in place.

"Unfortunately, the legislation was not worded in such a way that it could guarantee incrementality," he says. "If there was a flaw or chink in it, that was it. Incrementality was achieved with a number of provinces, but with the big province of Ontario, we didn't get much incrementality there. The Privy Council Office was expressing a lot of concern over that point, but if you don't have the policy or the legislative construct to make it happen, it's difficult."

The August Personage points out a more subtle issue. Even in provinces where the Foundation did achieve apparent incrementality, its contributions probably relieved the provinces of any need to increase their own student aid budgets. Over the years, then, the Foundation's bursaries may have suppressed provincial spending on student financial aid, thus creating a kind of tacit displacement that may well have grown as the years went by. This tacit displacement may have been one of the Foundation's most disappointing failures, though it is all but invisible to the casual observer.

The Foundation's agreements with the provinces, however, reflected the principles that in 1999 formed the basis for

61

the Social Union Framework Agreement between Ottawa and the provinces. As the government's own Social Union website explains, the agreement declares that "Each provincial and territorial government will determine the detailed program design and mix best suited to its own needs and circumstances to meet the agreed objectives. A provincial/territorial government which, because of its existing programming, does not require the total transfer to fulfill the agreed objectives would be able to reinvest any funds not required for those objectives in the same or a related priority area."

The federal expectation clearly was that all the Foundation's money would be incremental, but the actual award letters sent out to bursary recipients, says Alex Usher, simply said, "'Here's three thousand bucks'—and it was not real clear that because you were getting three thousand bucks from us, you might not be getting three thousand dollars from somebody else. Additionally—and we knew this, but the feds didn't seem to know it until it hit the headlines—there were some people who would have been made worse off by getting the award. That's because your three thousand dollars from us might have meant that you'd be getting three thousand dollars less in loan remission."

And why did that matter? Because, Usher says, the provinces tend not to issue income tax slips indicating that loan remission is taxable income—which it actually is—while the Foundation was required to issue income tax slips for its bursaries. The outcome for the student was that $3,000 of tax-free loan remission had been replaced by $3,000 of taxable bursary. When students figured that out, they held angry press conferences denouncing the bursary program and rejecting their bursaries—a far cry from the wave of gratitude that the government had been expecting.

"So in the 2000 budget the federal government hastily brought in a $3,000 exemption for bursaries," Usher says. "But in the meantime there had been a lot of bad headlines about it."

JEAN LAPIERRE was a tall, self-confident, worldly man of fifty when he was hired in April 1999 to manage the Foundation's communications program. At that point, the Foundation consisted of Norman Riddell; the chief financial officer, Paul Bourque; an administrative officer; and a secretary and receptionist, Maria Modafferi. Lapierre quickly realized that because of the tensions around the Foundation's creation, especially in Quebec, a traditional corporate communications program made no sense.

"The more we did communication, the worse was our reputation," he explains. "So my first suggestion to the director was to stop doing communications and to build our activities, get some results, and start doing communications again after that." Journalists, he remarks, were never really captivated by stories about student loans and grants, nor did they respond well to good-news stories. So it made more sense to focus on government relations, on publications, on relations between the Foundation and the students, and their families.

Lapierre organized his own department along the same lines as the Foundation itself. He would have a small staff to respond to correspondence and to edit, translate, release and promote the Foundation's publications—a job that expanded dramatically as the Foundation's research effort grew. But most communications services would be provided by contractors spread out across the country.

"Instead of hiring people, I hired outside service providers," he says. "I had two things in mind here. The first one was

63

to avoid dictating from Montreal what was efficient in eastern Canada or western Canada. The idea was to connect with local needs or aspirations by using local or regional organizations. So we have seven outside service providers—in Halifax, Montreal, Toronto, in the Prairies, and in Alberta and in B.C. And on top of that we have another one that deals only with aboriginals.

"The second objective was to avoid having a big staff sitting here waiting for orders. This way, each individual job may cost more, but overall we thought it would cost less. For example, these organizations are presently organizing what we call LG ceremonies. We partner with lieutenant governors' offices, and we hold events all across the country where they invite all our entrance award and In-course award recipients, and their families, to a reception.

"Now we don't have the contacts with all those LG offices. And just having a staff from Montreal travelling to all those cities, meeting people, arranging those events, renting hotel rooms, hiring caterers, attending those meetings—that would cost a lot of money. But the outside service providers are already there. They have the contacts, they make it happen and they do it all for $5,000. Well, just the airfares to do it from Montreal would cost more than this."

One of the difficulties of doing communications for the Foundation is the near-impossibility of talking in any concrete way about the overwhelming majority of the students aided by the Foundation. What defines eligibility for 95 per cent of the Foundation's grants is need, and considerations of privacy mean that the Foundation cannot identify those students. These issues may even have contributed to the Foundation's eventual demise.

"I always felt that if we could not portray the Foundation as an organization that was helping needy people, we would not get renewed," says Jean Lapierre. "But we weren't capable of portraying ourselves as the organization created by the government for that purpose. We portrayed ourselves as a research organization, we portrayed ourselves as an excellence award organization, but we were never able to portray ourselves as helping needy students."

Norman Riddell agrees.

"We were always constrained in talking about bursary winners because they get their grants on the basis of need," he explains. "So if I start talking about individuals, I'm announcing to the world that they're needy. It's like taking your social assistance recipients and holding them up in a press conference. It never seemed right to do that. If the students chose to make the fact that they received a Millennium bursary public, fine. But it was not our place to make it public."

In fact, as Jean Lapierre points out, nobody gets praised for providing student aid—not the provinces, not the federal government, not the universities, not the other foundations in the field. The same thing applies to many government programs; once they're established, they become—like student aid—just something that people expect to be provided. If the federal government were to add $50 million a year to student aid, says Lapierre, nobody would really notice, let alone applaud.

And doesn't the fact that the Foundation delivers its bursaries through the provincial student aid offices—and even uses the province's application forms—mean that many students don't even know that the Foundation has supported them? Lapierre nods his head vigorously.

"The vast majority!" he says. The information may be on the actual cheques, but, he shrugs, "we're all the same. We just cash the cheque. We don't look on the tab to see who's participating in the funding. We just cash the cheque."

For reasons that were obscure to Lapierre, Riddell also

handed him the responsibility for operating some access programs himself. (The reason, Riddell later explained, is that these are more communications programs than access programs, and Lapierre is in charge of communications.) In 2004, consultations around a major evaluation of the Foundation revealed a great deal of confusion among students and parents about various sources of student aid, and also about the costs and benefits of higher education. High school students generally get terrible information about post-secondary education, don't know what's available to them and rely on their parents for help. But the parents commonly know even less than the children. Based on this compounded ignorance and misinformation, students are expected to make informed and rational choices about their own education.

Norman Riddell found himself in Victoria discussing these matters with Tom Vincent, the assistant deputy minister of higher education. Vincent nodded, remarking that he was well aware of the problem and had some money available to improve the transition to post-secondary study. Riddell went home to Montreal and told Lapierre he wanted to have a project put together in two to three weeks. Lapierre turned to an outside service provider, developed the project and had it approved by the board in six weeks. Tom Vincent also approved, and the resulting program, Perspectives, is now available in all schools in British Columbia and was expected to be offered by other provinces in the fall of 2010.

Lapierre administers a second awareness program specifically for aboriginal people in northern Saskatchewan. At the outset, the Foundation's board included two very strong aboriginal members: Phil Fontaine, National Chief of the Assembly of First Nations, and cultural entrepreneur and philanthropist

66

John Kim Bell. Fontaine and Bell argued strongly that a portion of the Foundation's scholarships should be specifically allocated to aboriginal students. The board decided against it, but instead voted to authorize special communications programs for native communities.

Throughout his tenure at the Foundation, Jean Lapierre attempted to increase the number of aboriginal students who applied for bursaries and Excellence Awards. His last initiative involved mobilizing teachers in fifty-five or sixty schools in northern Saskatchewan to inform their students about the Foundation's programs and about other opportunities for higher education. Ideally, he would have liked to see all of the provinces adopting a version of the Perspectives program designed specifically for aboriginal students, but he was nevertheless happy to have convinced the federal and provincial governments to design a pan-Canadian Perspectives resource that includes interviews with aboriginal students.

The idea, he says, is "to create role models in the aboriginal communities, and peer relationships between aboriginal students and non-aboriginals and elders, so that we can talk about the realities of the school system and about the environment that other aboriginals found in the residential schools, universities and large cities. How is it to be away from their families and their cultural values and all these kinds of things?"

In Lapierre's view, the Foundation could and should have done more for aboriginal students. If the bursaries were to be allocated to the people with the greatest need, surely aboriginal students would be at the head of the list—but very few received Foundation support.

"I struggled for ten years to develop projects for them," Lapierre says. "There are many barriers. The main barrier is not the money. You know, any aboriginal child who says, 'I want to go to school' has probably an aunt or an uncle or somebody in the family who was in residential schools. We know the importance of parental influence of kids when they're at a young age. So what kind of message will they give?

"I think we have to do something as a country. We have to genuinely try to look at the society we have created and what pains these people have. We tried for two hundred years to oppress them and assimilate them. It doesn't work. We end up with melancholy people or people that live on the street. They are in very bad shape."

The situation of aboriginal people has become something of a personal mission for Jean Lapierre, and he hoped to work in that field after the Foundation closed, trying to help aboriginal families to feel more at ease with the educational system—not only the public schools, but also the universities, the trade schools, the colleges.

"That comes from visiting aboriginals and seeing how crazy the system is," he reflects. "Working at the Foundation I was trying to help aboriginals to get our money to go to an institution, and we know that those institutions are not organized to serve the needs of aboriginal people. They were built for middle-class white people, who are much more individualistic, for example. So I realized that pushing aboriginal people in the current school system may be a profound mistake, because we may just raise their level of frustration. If we push them in and after three months they drop out, they will be more averse to the school system.

"My view is more and more that we should try to create a pathway where we could support or accompany aboriginal students for a while, try to bring them in a channel where it would always be safe for them. If I were able to do something of that sort I would be very happy. The issue is about the core of the society. We will never be the country we could be if we don't fix this."

There is a certain logic in Jean Lapierre's involvement with the aboriginal projects he supervised for the Foundation, and they certainly fit his passion, if not his job description. Still, they were a long way from traditional corporate communications. Both could as easily have been developed as pilot projects administered by the research section. Why didn't it work out that way? Lapierre gave an eloquent Gallic shrug.

"Normally these should have been pilot projects," he said. "At that time I didn't know whether M. Riddell felt it was more or less communications, or he felt the research people had enough on their plate, or whatever. But this is the pragmatic aspect of this organization. It doesn't run necessarily in a linear fashion."

Lapierre frowned for a moment, trying to formulate an idea. His corner office at the Foundation was lined with music CDs, ship models and works of art. An electronic piano lay discreetly under its dust cover. Perhaps it caught his eye. He came up with a striking analogy.

"My understanding is this," he says. "M. Riddell had a certain number of keys on his keyboard—he is a pianist—and he wanted this kind of tone, and if he thought he was going to get it from this person, he went to them. If he thought he was going to get it from me, he came to me. That's the way he liked to run the business.

"I'm not sure I can exactly explain it, but I play the piano as well, and I know that you don't necessarily play the piano the same way if you want different colours. With Rachmaninoff you won't play the notes the same way as if you played Debussy, for example. I think M. Riddell played the organization this way. Sometimes he liked to play slightly in a different way, to get a different nuance.

"He has a sort of creativity like you would get in a small enterprise, with a small entrepreneur who feels the deal, feels how the product should be made—sometimes he makes mistakes, sometimes it's a big success—but real entrepreneurs, they don't understand exactly, they just *feel* the market, they *feel* the niche or the customers. I think Riddell has this kind of a nose, and he's very good at this kind of thing."

THE MILLENNIUM Bursary Program, which represented 95 per cent of the Foundation's grants, was like a Manitoba farm combine—a vast juggernaut mowing a swath as wide as a city park, controlled by operators who were dwarfed by the apparatus they were steering. From coast to coast, the bursaries were distributed to roughly 120,000 students annually—a number comparable to the population of Kingston, Trois-Rivières or Kelowna. The amount totalled nearly $335 million a year, which would constitute more than 20 per cent of the provincial budget of Prince Edward Island. Over its lifetime, the Foundation, which started with $2.5 billion, actually distributed about $3.3 billion. The extra $800 million came from a shrewd investment program overseen by Paul Bourque, supported by three investment managers and board member Margot Ritchie, a partner in the investment firm of Jarislowsky Fraser. The Foundation did not suffer a major loss in the market meltdown of 2008.

And because it was run in cooperation with the provinces and made use of provincial staff and infrastructure wherever possible, the Foundation's whole staff for the Millennium Bursary Program consisted of three people, with some assistance from three or four more. The manager was Randolf Harrold. He and his administrative assistant were supported by a handful of other people in finance and operations who also handled all the rest of the Foundation's business affairs.

An international trade expert, economist and business development consultant, Randolf Harrold had worked with Norman Riddell in the Canadian diplomatic service and also in the government of Saskatchewan, where both were deputy ministers. There they were involved with the Meech Lake Accord and also the North American Free Trade Agreement. Harrold subsequently served in trade and economic development positions with both the federal government and the Province of Nova Scotia. After taking early retirement, he went to work for Dalhousie University doing commercialization of new technology as the CEO of Nova Universities Technology Inc., an initiative of Dalhousie and the Nova Scotia Agricultural College.

In 2002, he got a call from Riddell, who was by then the CEO of the Canada Millennium Scholarship Foundation. The Foundation's task, Riddell explained, was to deliver federally funded bursaries to students by means of partnerships with the provinces. Riddell needed someone with federal–provincial experience to manage the bursary program and to help with the development of better relations with the provinces. Would Harrold be available? He would.

"I was quite overwhelmed at first by the number of agreements and all the bureaucratic functions that had to be managed in terms of the databases and programs and so on," Harrold recalls. "We got 35,000 names from Ontario, for example, every November and my job was to analyze this list of names, make sure everybody met the criteria of the awards, and then draw up resolutions for the board and have all those people approved.

"Ontario was 38 per cent of our business, and there it was a straightforward transfer to the province, so it was a single cheque and a single list. In Saskatchewan, on the other hand, we had Aboriginal Access and that could be paid three different times a year, because the program had three forms, which meant three lists with three different formulas. That's just one program, and we had two more of those in Manitoba and several others elsewhere."

Despite the complexity, however, he found that the partnerships with the provinces greatly simplified the operation.

"We got lists of students from the provinces every year, listing the eligible students in rank order of their financial need as assessed by the provincial student financial assistance program. This turned out to be quite a boon administratively. It was all highly computerized, so all we had to do was set up programs to assess these lists and pass them for approval to our board."

One of the routine checks on the provincial lists—easily done from the databases—was to ensure that the same students weren't applying for assistance simultaneously in more than one province. Every year, a handful of students tried that—and would have gotten away with it but for the Foundation's systems, since the provinces have no ability to cross-check one another's records.

The overall arrangement made the Foundation "increasingly able to make adjustments to fit the program needs of individual provinces, because we did have these separate agreements with them." Some provinces decided to change the criteria for their bursaries in mid-stream, while others—notably British Columbia, Manitoba, Ontario and Nova Scotia—collaborated with the Foundation to put additional funds into what then became joint grant programs. And, says Harrold, "because we were able to work with the provinces to tailor these agreements and target the assistance more to their specific needs, they came to be very receptive to the core program."

Harrold's responsibilities also included direct contact and problem-solving with bursary recipients. He answered, he reckoned, about 130 emails every week and frequently called students to resolve their issues directly. He found these things time consuming, but also very satisfying. And he agreed that many students were never even aware that the Foundation had helped them.

"We had an obligation under the law to inform students where the money was coming from," he reflects, "and so we sent every student a letter at the time they received the awards. But it didn't strike deep into the consciousness of a lot of students, I don't suppose, and so there are a lot who didn't realize how much had flowed their way."

But when students did realize what had been provided, they could be almost painfully grateful. Reading their comments, getting an idea of their passion, their effort and their gratitude, is a humbling experience.

My financial situation was looking so dire that I was looking at having to withdraw from Law School. Working three part-time jobs and carrying a full course load has affected my health to the point of both mental and physical exhaustion. I have not had the luxury of a weekend off in 3 years . . . It has been really tough going. So thank you once again from the bottom of my heart.

Thanks for helping me have an amazing four years. I have made two movies with friends, learned to throw a disc forehand, scrubbed an elephant and caught my dream of medicine.

Life has not been easy as a single parent and the decision to return to school to get educated and have an opportunity of a career as a legal assistant was not an easy decision to make due to financial reasons. The student loan that I have barely covers our living expenses for me and my daughter. To know that when I finish school I will not owe as much because of the Millennium Foundation is such an incentive to me and a gift. I have been working very hard . . . Thank you again for your help.

Returning to school as a disabled student has presented many challenges and many rewards. Moving towards professional qualification that will allow me to play a contributing role in our society while establishing financial stability for myself is a dream come true. I can barely express the joy I experience in moving towards these accomplishments or gratitude I feel to all those who have played essential roles in these developments.

This could not have come at a better time. I won't go into details much, but my house burned down a couple of months back, I maxed my Visa in order to drive from Yellowknife to Ottawa to go to school and I haven't been able to pay off my tuition because of lots of different financial difficulties. This is a godsend.

Thank you so much for allowing me to receive a Millennium Scholarship. My university college does not have a residence so I have to be in an apartment. My home town is 400 km away. With the vacancy rate so low, the rents are exorbitant and so I have two jobs to keep up . . . Thank you again.

I am taking my third year in my professional degree as a pastor . . . Besides my school work, I am looking after my mother, age

74

77; and my two aunts, age 82 and 88. I also work at a seniors' home, an orphanage, at a hospital, and on Saturday and Sundays, I am a youth pastor at a church . . . My goal now is to finish my education and start serving the community.

Before my parents' divorce in 1992, my father left us with no financial resources. He even withdrew my education fund which, unfortunately, listed him as the owner of the policy . . . Not only was Mom left with no finances and no pension, she was diagnosed with breast cancer a year and a half before the divorce . . .

As a single mother, a recent immigrant and a student, I cannot begin to express the appreciation that I felt when I received your Bursary. I hope to someday make my country, Canada, proud of my achievements and help its development in both the informatics and health fields.

Writing to the Foundation after graduation, one student suddenly realized what she had received, and was overwhelmed.

Hi there,
I just got off the phone with Manitoba Student Aid. I'm doing my taxes for the first time since 2004, now of course that I'm no longer a student. The woman on the phone told me how many Millennium Scholarships I received and for how much. I wrote down one, then two, then she listed another. Three years, totalling $10,571. I was speechless. I started tearing up.

When I was in school and so busy, so broke, so hungry, I would get these letters, and because all things to do with money then were a blur to me (too stressful to think about!), I don't think it ever really hit me what they were for, what they were doing.

75

And now, having worked in the world for a year, my school years behind me, and listening to the woman at Manitoba Student Aid tell me these amounts . . . What your program did for me with those bursaries, what those bursaries do for me now . . . I am lost for words.

Thank you so, so, so, very much for supporting students like me. While most of them, like me, probably don't realize what you're doing for them at the time, they will soon. And then just like that, in a swift, profound moment, they'll realize what you're doing—is everything; what you're giving—is everything.

Please tell everyone there that the work you do is not simply work. It is never just work, and will never be.

IN 2002, Jean Monty abruptly resigned from six of the eight boards on which he served, including the boards of BCE and the Canada Millennium Scholarship Foundation. Under his leadership, in pursuit of a strategy called "convergence," stodgy old Bell Canada had transformed itself from a telephone company to a go-go multimedia giant, controlling CTV television, Teleglobe, the *Globe and Mail* and various cable and online enterprises. In the wake of the dot-com meltdown, however, convergence was beginning to look like an idea whose time might never come, and Monty was fully occupied dealing with the fallout.

His replacement as chair of the Foundation's board was Gérard Veilleux, a career public servant who had worked in the governments of Manitoba, Quebec and Canada. In Ottawa, Veilleux had been deputy clerk of the Privy Council, secretary to the cabinet for Federal-Provincial Relations, secretary of the Treasury Board and president of the Canadian Broadcasting Corporation. He moved to the private sector in 1994 as president of Power Communications, part of the Desmarais empire in Montreal. He had been a friend of Prime Minister Chrétien for forty years; the two of them had met in the 1960s, when the nearly unilingual young Chrétien was parliamentary secretary to the Minister of Finance, and Veilleux was one of the very few francophones in the department.

Monty had been a strong, decisive but somewhat Olympian chair, very forceful and influential at a macro level, but quite detached from the daily operations of the organization. As an alumnus of private schools himself, Monty owed no personal gratitude to the public educational system, and as a prominent player in "Quebec, Inc." he had taken some risks in chairing a federally chartered organization—but he had done it as a public service, and as a gesture of corporate citizenship on behalf of a major public company.

Veilleux, however, identified with the Foundation's mission in a deep and visceral way. A native of the hard-scrabble mining town of Asbestos, Quebec, Veilleux—like Chrétien—had gained his education through diligence and determination and with a great deal of support from others, and he knew that his education had shaped his entire life. The youngest of five children, Veilleux was only five years old when his father died, at which point his seventeen-year-old brother quit school and went to work to support the family.

"I'm going to tell you something very personal," Veilleux says softly. "My brother only told me this just before he died, quite recently. After he went to work, he went to talk with my mother, and he said, 'We've got to do something for the little fellow'— which was me. He said, 'We've got to save a little money so we can send him to school. If we do five dollars a week, for ten to twelve years, we're going to have our $12,000 and he can go to school.' This was 1947. Five dollars a week.

"So they saved the money. And then Mother, through a bad set of circumstances, remarried—and the money vanished with the new husband. I never knew it existed. My brother said, 'But you know, it turned out to be okay anyway, because you paid your own way through school and you got scholarships and student assistance.'"

An amazing story.

"Yes," Veilleux says quietly. "A story of grace. Generosity. Vision. He was always very proud of his little brother, and that was a great motivator for me. I didn't want to disappoint him."

Veilleux proved to be an exceptionally supportive leader for the board, hearing people out, seeking consensus, involving individual members more deeply in the Foundation's work. He could be firm when he needed to be, but as Norman Riddell put it, "the board *grew* under Gérard." His commitment was very personal, and he made a habit of dropping by the Foundation's offices, which were only a few blocks from his own, and walking around and talking with people. He came to know the operation very well, and Riddell found him an invaluable sounding board when he needed to discuss personnel issues on a confidential basis. He had a strong concern for the people who worked for the Foundation, and they in turn became very comfortable with him.

Which is not to suggest that he intruded on the sphere of management. His approach to the Foundation, he says, reflected his experience at the Power Corporation group, a family business with "a very long-term culture." Among its principles: "You let your managers manage. You make sure you hire the right people. You are active on the boards. You develop good operational and strategic plans, and they stick to that. And you reward them if they meet their objectives.

"That's the way we operate here. And that's exactly how the Foundation operated, too. And it works tremendously well."

Veilleux was appointed in 2002 for a five-year term without remuneration. He considered his appointment to be a great honour, a chance to pay back his country in a modest way, and he was deeply touched. In 2007, however, when his term expired, the government had changed, and Veilleux received a form letter saying that his order-in-council appointment had expired, and thank you very much for serving. Goodbye.

"A little cavalier," he says. "Very cavalier, in fact. My mother would have said *mal élevé*—badly raised." But the law provides that in such circumstances, the incumbent continues to serve until a replacement is named, and the government didn't get around to appointing a replacement for another two years, so Veilleux served until late 2008. Given that the Foundation was closing, it wasn't easy to find a replacement for him, and eventually the members of the board concluded that it would be best to appoint someone already serving on the board. They proposed Dr. Paule Leduc as the new chair, and the government accepted the suggestion.

Dr. Leduc had then served on the board for eight years. She had enjoyed a distinguished career as an academic, an administrator and a civil servant. Having grown up in a small village in the Saguenay region of Quebec, she had overcome numerous obstacles—including cash, class and gender—en route to attaining a Ph.D. in French literature from the Université de Paris. Her subsequent career included fifteen years as a deputy minister in the Quebec ministries of Intergovernmental Affairs, International Relations and Cultural Affairs. She had also served as director of the Canada Council for the Arts and president of the Social Sciences and Humanities Research Council of Canada.

When the Foundation was established, she was rector of the Université du Québec à Montréal, and therefore, she says, "part of the gang" of Quebec university presidents who opposed this new federal initiative, dismayed that so much money was going to a newly created organization. Once the issues with Quebec had been resolved, however, and it was clear that the Foundation's Millennium Bursary Program would indeed provide additional funds to Quebec students, she was comfortable joining the board.

Dr. Leduc had been a Quebec deputy minister during the constitutional negotiations of 1987 when the province had been pushing for a more decentralized federation—but decentralization, she smiles, was "not the philosophy of the year in Ottawa." She joined the board realizing that the Foundation was attempting to do federalism in a different way, and she was curious to see how the experiment would work. She found it to be "an extraordinary experience, a perfect example of decentralization, an example that shows it can work."

She notes wryly that the Foundation's successor program, the new Canada Student Grants Program, has apparently reverted to the old one-size-fits-all model, which probably means that Quebec will not participate. She is not surprised. The flexibility of asymmetrical federalism, she says, "is not in the genetics of the federal government." All the same, she hopes that policy-makers both in the provinces and in Ottawa have been paying attention to the Foundation's "very important achievement" in showing a different way to manage the federation.

80 THE APPOINTMENT of a new chair in 2002 was not the only significant mid-term development in the Foundation's evolution. Between its fourth and fifth anniversaries, said the legislation that created it, the Foundation "shall cause a review and report to be made of its activities and organization." In short, a mid-term review, to take place in 2003. But, says Andrew Parkin, "mid-term review" was a bit of a misnomer.

"The review was five years into the mandate, going back to its creation in 1998," he explains. "Well, there were no staff until 1999, and there were no awards until 2000, so if you have to publish a review in 2003, you're essentially looking at 2000, 2001, 2002. So it was really a review of the set-up and the first three years of operation. And the people who wrote it, when they were trying to answer the question, 'How are we doing?' basically came back and said, 'We can't really tell very much.'"

The review was conducted by the Institute of Intergovernmental Relations at Queen's University, drawing on the talents and knowledge of analysts and researchers from across the country. Overall, it found the Foundation to be an "innovative, well-managed organization," and it commended the Foundation on its financial management, its Excellence Awards and the policy relevance of its research program—though it noted that some observers saw the research program as inappropriate, a manifestation of "mandate creep." It noted that the Foundation thought it was "province-friendly," but that not all provinces agreed.

The review also questioned the basic premise of the bursary program, asking whether reducing the debt of existing students really was the most effective way to improve access—a fundamental question that the Foundation's own research was also addressing. The reviewers did not think the Foundation had fully resolved the issue of displacement, and they suggested that the impact of the bursary program might have been greater if— rather than reducing student debt—the bursaries had provided the student with additional immediate cash.

With the evaluation report in hand, the Foundation organized an eighteen-city cross-country consultation, soliciting the views of five hundred people at meetings and another 250 by email.

"We took the results of all these consultations," says Randolf Harrold, "and pretty well everyone said that we were not reaching students from low-income backgrounds very effectively. That was largely because students from low-income backgrounds often went to community colleges or other institutions that were nearby. And also the original Millennium Bursary Program didn't target first-year students. There were so many dropouts that most of the provinces thought the program should start in the second year and beyond." But that exclusion had turned out to be a mistake.

The feedback from the Queen's review and the national consultations prompted the Foundation to make significant changes in its programs. First, the main bursary program was extended to include first year, which meant that the Foundation could now assist many low-income students who had previously been left out because they were taking two-year programs at community colleges.

Next, the Foundation's management assessed their financial situation and determined that because the original $2.5-billion endowment had been well invested, its resources included $250 million more than originally expected. That meant the Foundation was in a position to create a new program of bursaries directed specifically at low-income students. And this time, having learned from its experiences, the Foundation was much bolder in tailoring the new Access Bursary Program to the individual provinces.

"One of the lessons that the Foundation had learned," Andrew Parkin remarks, "is that [the] situation of the provinces is very different in terms of the profile of their students, and the way their existing policies work. So the best way to make use of the new money was to adapt to both of those realities. What do the students need? And what is already being covered by other pro-grams? And the answers to both those questions will be different from jurisdiction to jurisdiction. So how you use your money to add on top of that will be different, too."

How different? Essentially, the Foundation ended up nego-tiating thirteen agreements and thirteen different programs, one with each province and territory. Some are quite similar, but several are very different. Alberta, for instance, had done some of its own access research and had specifically identified rural students as a priority. The Foundation was very comfort-able accepting the province's data and priorities, and because the province was also prepared to participate financially, the result was a joint program, which was unveiled at a ceremony in Red Deer rather than Edmonton.

Saskatchewan, however, wanted its access program directed specifically towards aboriginals. And Manitoba, which also has a large aboriginal population, chose to target high school drop-outs, or "adult learners," people who are completely out of the formal educational system—many of whom are also aborigi-nal. Nova Scotia's Access Bursary Program sent student aid officials out to the secondary schools, debunking myths about post-secondary education and promoting the fact that upfront cash grants were now available to low-income students. In Que-bec, the money that in other provinces was dedicated to new Access Bursary Programs was instead used by the government to resolve the 2005 conflict over loan ceilings.

Andrew Parkin vividly remembers the negotiation for the Access Bursaries in Ontario.

"Ontario had commissioned a report on its post-secondary education system, and among the things recommended in that report was that they should have a certain type of access bursary

for low-income students, which is exactly what we were also trying to do," he says. "And so I went to see Richard Jackson, the
head of the Ontario Student Assistance Program, and we had a
conversation along the lines of, 'Look, we have money that we
want to put into the Ontario system and you have this new report
that's urging you to retool your student financial aid system.
These don't have to be different things. You can decide what you
want to do, and then we can be a partner in trying to do that.'

"Richard basically paused and said, 'Do you mean we could
essentially use your money to help us do our thing?' And I said,
'Yeah.' They were supposed to bring in their new policy in '06,
and he already knew how much it was going to cost. But now he
realized that with our money also on the table, he could do it in
'05—and in '06 he could do more on top of that. And it could be
the same program.

"I don't want to exaggerate how dramatic it was, but I was trying to bring the message that we can be part of your solution, we
don't have to be this problem that you've got to deal with while
you're also trying to deal with this major recommendation. And
he got that message. He just realized that he had a lot more creative freedom now."

When it came time to write the actual agreement, Jackson
and an associate flew to Montreal, where they met with Parkin
and a colleague. The four sat in the boardroom for a day and
wrote the agreement.

"We ordered in barbeque chicken," Parkin recalls, "and we just
sat there with two computers open and wrote it out, because they
were going to announce it in their budget, and they had to have
enough certainty that it was going to work. After that there was
review and refinement on both sides, but for the basic core thing,
it just took four people in a room to sit there for a day and work
it out. For a $45-million program that would run for four years."

Implementing all these agreements was Randolf Harrold's job. He remembers Andrew Parkin walking into his office from time to time and handing him a new memorandum of understanding (MOU) with yet another province. Adding the new ones to the original ones, Harrold wound up administering twenty-seven different MOUS.

The other great difference between the original set of bursaries and the new Access Bursaries was the inclusion of a research and evaluation component right in the design of the new program. As Parkin explains, attempts to evaluate programs after the fact are often stymied because the most useful information was never collected and thus cannot be tabulated. This time, the research design was integrated into the program and negotiated with the provinces as part of the overall package.

"I think that was a distinctive value of the Foundation—that everything you did, you did in a way that you could learn the most about it, and you could report on its impact," Parkin reflects. "And that, as far as I know, had never been done before. That gets to another fundamental feature of the Foundation, namely that the Foundation had done a lot of good things because it didn't have time to waste. The research component of the Access Bursaries is a perfect example. This was going to be a four-year program and it was run between '05 and '09, at which point we would be finished, gone. So we couldn't wait till '08 to figure out how you might want to evaluate it. It had to be done all at once."

IN THE early days, the Foundation toyed with the idea of fundraising, putting together some funding that would allow it to continue and expand its programs independent of government—but the universities bristled at the very idea that the Foundation might also go trolling in the little pond of

Canadian philanthropy, and the notion soon disappeared. The Foundation did, however, conclude one very satisfactory partnership with a completely non-governmental organization.

The World Petroleum Congress is a major international meeting of oil companies, environmental organizations, ministers of oil, policy-makers in international organizations and other important players in the oil and gas industry. It is held every three years in different locations around the world, and each meeting is organized by the local branch of the World Petroleum Council, an international organization, based in London, England, with eighty member countries. In 2000, the congress was held in Calgary.

After the Calgary Congress, the Canadian organizing committee had $5 million left over and decided to use $4.2 million on scholarships for students in programs of study relevant to the industry, which might help address its looming labour shortage. It chose the Canada Millennium Scholarship Foundation to administer the scholarships.

The Foundation then negotiated memorandums of understanding with forty-nine Canadian post-secondary institutions that offered courses in oil-related subjects. It awarded about two hundred WPC bursaries annually, and the process was almost completely automated. Only students who received Millennium bursaries were eligible, which ensured that the chosen students had been identified as having financial need. Every year, the Foundation drew from its database of bursary recipients the names of students in the target disciplines studying in those forty-nine institutions. It sent the lists of names to the institutions, which sent back the students' grades. The Foundation selected the top two hundred and gave each one a bursary.

I am currently in third year Chemical Engineering Program. I came from Afghanistan about seven years ago and started school from Grade 9 with no elementary education. I was not able to speak a word of English at that time, but I learned that with hard work I can accomplish anything. I studied very hard to get into university so that I can build a future for myself. A future that I would have never been able to have being in the Afghanistan and also a woman. But getting into university came with another obstacle. That was how would I even be able to pay for my education? I cannot thank you enough for the financial assistance you provided. I hope one day I will be able to help students achieve their goals just as you have helped me.

"I thought there should be some kind of recognition for the students," says Randolf Harrold, whose office administered the WPC scholarships. "These are very interesting young people who were selected, at least in part, for their academic performance. So we set up recognition ceremonies and invited members of the petroleum industry to come and meet the students, and all this grew into a process that I set up—a little program called the Student Industry Opportunities Program. Over the years we have held these ceremonies in a number of centres, including Calgary, Toronto, Montreal and St. John's. The students were recognized for their achievements, and they were introduced to industry members and could network with them. We set up a website where the students could post their resumes and HR people from the oil companies in the industry could look at them, and so on.

"Well, this grew into an interest by the World Petroleum Council, who asked me to come to one of their council meetings and make presentations. Now they've replicated this program in a number of other countries as a legacy of the Congress, so there's one in Brazil, one in South Africa, one in Norway and one in Spain."

The industry, Harrold says, has recognized that even as it expands, many of its key employees are reaching retirement age, and young people are not particularly enthusiastic about their industry. As a result, the Congress now includes a social responsibility and environmental component, which in turn includes a youth forum focused on issues that are barriers for youth to choosing a career in the industry—issues like climate change, alternate technologies, emission reductions, sustainability and environmental stewardship.

The Foundation, says Norman Riddell, was an instrument of change. Well, yes. Still, one would hardly have guessed that it would eventually conjure up sister programs in Africa and South America, all funded by the petroleum industry.

> The Odyssey of Christian Hamuli

. . . .

IN 1990, when Christian Hamuli was eighteen years old, government commandos attacked the University of Lubumbashi, where he was studying to be an engineer like his uncle. Lubumbashi is the second-largest city in the Democratic Republic of Congo (DRC), which was then ruled by Joseph Mobutu, a particularly corrupt and vicious dictator. Mobutu later renamed himself Mobutu Sese Seko Nkuku Ngbendu Wa Za Banga: the all-powerful warrior who, through will and endurance, goes from conquest to conquest leaving fire in his wake. Supported by the United States because he opposed communism, the all-powerful warrior ruled for thirty-two bloody years.

But he was afraid of ideas, and therefore of students and teachers.

"Mobutu was actually obsessed with university students," Christian explains. "Universities have free speech, and they have young people that are exposed to political science and learning new things and how the world is different from where they live. They start seeing flaws in the system, and then they rebel. And sometimes they have politicians who like to have their support. So that is dangerous to someone like Mobutu."

Christian survived the attack and returned to his studies a year later when the university was reopened. Three years later, however, his family was attacked, and his only brother—just fifteen years old—was executed with a bullet to his forehead.

"It was such a blow to my beliefs in my own country that I couldn't stay in Congo anymore," he says. "That's when I said, 'No, this country is doomed'—and I left."

He made his way to Kenya, where he survived for a year and a half. He was arrested as an illegal immigrant and briefly jailed. ("You don't want to be in a jail in Kenya," he says softly. "Anything can happen.") A sympathetic Canadian suggested he move to Uganda because it would be easier to claim refugee status from a country that, unlike Kenya, borders on the DRC.

In Uganda, supporting himself as a French teacher, he applied as a refugee student for a visa to study engineering in Canada, but no Canadian engineering school would accept him. A friendly Canadian official, however, thought that Christian would adapt easily to Canada, and suggested that he apply as an immigrant worker.

"God bless that visa officer," says Christian. "But I didn't really believe her. And then one day I was teaching and my friend phoned me and said that my visa had come."

He landed in Edmonton. He was entitled to a year of public support while he oriented himself and made his way into the labour force, but after a month he went out, learned to write resumés, and got a job working in a laundry from 8:30 p.m. to 5:00 a.m.

"After six months I said, 'No, this is going to kill me intellectually.' I approached my manager and told him I wanted to go back to school." Instead, the manager promoted him and switched him to the day shift—but after a year Christian still wanted to go back to school. He enrolled in Grant MacEwan College in a university transfer program, studying in the evenings. He had been out of school for eight years.

It was hard, he says, living on a student loan in a country he didn't know very well, so he kept working at the laundry. He put in ten-hour shifts on Sundays, which made it hard to stay awake Monday in class. But he completed first-year engineering and transferred to the University of Alberta. In Africa, he had enrolled in civil engineering, which African countries desperately need, but now a fellow student suggested he think more about his future in Canada. So Christian switched to petroleum engineering.

At that point, says Randolf Harrold, he was "sort of skimming along academically, just barely making it over the trees. We gave him a Millennium Bursary; he qualified for that because he was borrowing money from the Alberta Student Aid and from Canada Student Loans. And then he was selected by the university in his third year for a World Petroleum Congress scholarship."

"In the mail they told me that I've been chosen for a scholarship," grins Christian. "That was a pleasing surprise. Oh, it was like an angel came up with this! It was more than I would make the whole year, working every Sunday. So why should I kill myself anymore? I have to focus now on school—and now I quit my part-time job."

As a WPC scholar, Christian was invited to address an industry conference in Montreal, where he met "a man of great spirit" named David Boone, an important player in the oil business. Boone, who remains a close friend and mentor, subsequently guided the young graduate to his present position with the

Alberta Energy and Utilities Board (EUB), which regulates the province's petroleum industry.

Christian Hamuli sits in the lobby of the EUB headquarters building in Calgary, smiling and talking about how he loves his job, how he loves to go to work in the morning. He recently married the daughter of another Congolese refugee, and after conferring with David Boone, he bought a house. He has just returned from his first visit to his parents in the DRC, and he is saddened by the state of his native country. He hopes to do something for the DRC some day. But he is living in the here and now, he hopes soon to start a family and, he says, "I wouldn't want to be in any other country than Canada."

> *four*

TO FOSTER EXCELLENCE

. . . .

"ONE OF the interviews I did," says Melissa Moi, an Excellence Awards officer with the Foundation, "was with this student in rural Alberta who was sixteen years old when his dad decided he couldn't afford to run the farm any more and had to take a job in Saskatchewan to support the family.

"But the son didn't want the farm to die, so he decided to manage it himself—at sixteen—including the two full-time employees. He was eighteen when he applied for the scholarship, and I got the sense from his letter of recommendation that he was already a solid pillar of this rural Alberta community."

He certainly was. After taking over the farm, Jared Foat did his schooling over the Internet for two and a half years and then returned to regular school. As a full time student, he was a member of the student council, captain of both the hockey team and the volleyball team and president of the local 4-H club. Through 4-H, he put on a series of public speaking workshops for students and parents, because he understood the need for people to improve their communication skills in order to be involved with their communities.

His dream was to own and operate the family farm near Carstairs, Alberta, but his father insisted that he qualify for a lucrative alternative profession before taking on the risky career of farming. Jared decided to become a chiropractor and wanted to take a pre-chiropractic course at Mount Royal College in Calgary—while continuing to manage the farm. (Running a farm, he shrugs, is mostly a summer job anyway.) He applied for a Millennium Excellence Award.

"So I called to interview him," says Melissa. "His mom thought I was a friend and said, 'He's out with the cows, dear!' I told her who I was, and I said, 'How long is he going to be out there?' And she said 'Well, it depends on how healthy they are. I don't know. But you can try on his cell phone. And if he's not too busy with the cows he'll be able to answer.'"

And that, says Melissa, is the kind of person who would win an Excellence Award from the Foundation. It wasn't just a question of marks, though a first-rate academic record certainly mattered. Fundamentally, though, the Excellence Awards were about character, imagination, dedication and leadership.

"This scholarship rewarded people who had seen a need in their community and reacted to it, and made a significant differ-ence," says Melissa. "I used to say, 'These aren't Canada's future leaders. These are leaders in Canada right now.'"

THE MILLENNIUM Excellence Award Program can almost be seen as the tail that wagged the Foundation dog. It disbursed only 5 per cent of the Foundation's student assistance, but as Norman Riddell remarked, it was a labour-intensive program, employing 25 per cent of the Foundation's staff. It was the only Millennium assistance program that had nothing to do with need. It was entirely a merit program, focused on finding outstanding Canadians of the next generation and supporting them not only with money, but also with a suite of programs designed to help them grow both as scholars and as leaders. Five per cent may not sound like much, but 5 per cent of $3 billion is $150 million, which represents more than 24,000 scholarships. That made the Excellence Awards the largest scholarship program in the country.

The director of the Excellence Awards Program was Andrew Woodall. The program, he says, was unique even in its design. There was nothing like it in Canada and there won't be anything like it again soon. Woodall says that "on paper it was elitist, because it was all about recognizing the 'best' students—but it wasn't that elitist, if you consider that it wasn't just the forty best students, it was the *two thousand* best students every year. That starts making you think about 'best' differently."

Boyish, warm and eager, Andrew may have worn a suit in the office, but he was distinctly happier in cargo pants and T-shirts at weekend conferences of students.

Voices in the air:

Andrew is very skilled at building authentic relationships, and that is how change happens.

Seeing his courage and his risk-taking has, I think, given me the courage to do the same.

Andrew jokes that he doesn't know how certain things work. You know he obviously does.

Yes, but he also knows how important it is for his employees to own what they do.

He has an unbelievably clear vision about how networks can work to enhance what you're doing.

At forty-four, Andrew was the Wise Old Counsellor of the excellence team. Many of his staffers were only a fraction of his age.

"They were young and they were really smart and they didn't suffer fools gladly," Andrew smiles, "so when you pushed them, they pushed you back—and sometimes they didn't know when to stop. But that's all right, because they pushed back in ways that showed they cared. They worked really hard, they gave a lot of themselves intellectually and emotionally, they were very dedicated. In fact, the most satisfying aspect of the job was working with the people I worked with."

He was, he says, constantly grateful for his team's competence and engagement and interest. His colleagues were "people that you want to know, people that you want to sit down with and talk with, not just work with." Their tasks with the Excellence Award program included the marketing, the application process, the evaluation process and the renewal process. One-third of the awards were renewable, and Andrew's team provided a range of ancillary programming for the students who held those renewable awards.

The Excellence Award program was designed by Franca Gucciardi, who was also its first director. But the first draft of the largest merit scholarship program in Canadian history was a failure. It called for a relatively small number of very large and prestigious "national" scholarships, amounting to as much as $40,000 over four years. That idea, however, ran straight up against the restrictions of the Foundation's governing legislation, which provided that no recipient of the Foundation's support could receive more than $15,000, plus inflation.

"We went to a couple of different law firms and said, 'Find us a way out of this $15,000 limit,'" Alex Usher remembers, "and they said, 'No, you can't.' We creatively reinterpreted a couple of things in terms of inflation and got it up to about $19,000." But that was that. The selection process had already begun, so the program had to be redesigned on the fly.

The program that emerged from the redesign was lean, sophisticated and elegant. Unlike most entrance awards, the Millennium Excellence Awards were not based solely on academic achievement, but also required evidence of leadership, community service, engagement and innovation. The plan was to award about one thousand scholarships every year, and they would come in three tiers. One hundred would be National Awards of $5,000, renewable for three years. Another two hundred students would win Provincial or Territorial Awards of $4,000, also renewable, while seven hundred Local Award winners would receive a one-time award of $4,000. National and Provincial Award winners would be known as "laureates."

The program would be promoted to high school students across the country. The applications would be read and ranked by local committees made up of qualified volunteers, who would be trained by the Foundation's staff. Franca and her staff would merge and massage the lists, and present the results to the board for final approval. Then the volunteers would phone the successful applicants to give them the good news.

And the whole operation would be managed, at least initially, by just two people: Franca Gucciardi and a young Acadian from New Brunswick named Stéphane LeBlanc.

"I came in on February 1, 2000," Stéphane remembers. "The Excellence Award Program had been designed, but it hadn't yet been launched. So we announced it to the public, and we launched the first application campaign. It was basically just us two. We travelled the country that first year to visit schools to market the program to students and teachers. It was quite an amazing year. There were six thousand high schools on our mailing list, and we went to as many as we could. We may have hit a couple of hundred, which is all we could do.

"We thought that if we got three thousand applications, or maybe five thousand, we would be ecstatic. Well, we actually got 7,600, and in later years we got eleven thousand. But the school visitation in that first year turned out to be a great thing, right? It really established our program from year 1 as one of the premier scholarship programs in the country."

To evaluate the applications, the program needed a large network of volunteer assessors. To find those volunteers, Franca drew on the network she had built up in her earlier career at the Canadian Merit Scholarship Foundation, and asked her contacts to pass the word to their own networks. She and Stéphane also approached high school guidance counsellors and circulated nomination forms to the Canadian Association of Student Financial Aid Administrators, with whom the Foundation had by then already developed a good working relationship. They wrote to organizations like the United Way, 4-H Canada and Scouts Canada. Eventually they had a network of about 125 volunteers working in twenty-one committees across the country, each one chaired by an administrator. In the last years of the Foundation, about 250 volunteers worked together in thirty-nine committees. Every application was read at least twice. Successful ones could be read by seven or eight different people.

Being an assessor was no small commitment. Jump cut: In a corner office on the twenty-first floor of Cathedral Place in downtown Vancouver, floor-to-ceiling windows give a view of glass towers and moored container ships, with the blue mountains of the offshore islands misty in the background. The office belongs to Peter Wong, vice-president of investment dealer Raymond James Ltd. One winter day in 2009, the man sitting at the desk was not Peter Wong, but a university student named Alvin Chung, and file folders were spread out across the whole floor of the office.

Alvin was helping Peter do a first cull through Millennium scholarship applications. Peter tiptoed between the file folders, taking calls on his smartphone while he fielded questions from his visitor. At forty-eight, he was a former chairman of the Dragon Boat Festival and a director of the Vancouver Art Gallery and the Dr. Sun Yat-Sen Garden in Chinatown. He had been an assessor for eight years.

"My first experience was working with Franca, and I've never seen anyone more passionate and intelligent and enthusiastic," he said. "And that just set the standard—you know, if I was going to be involved in this, I was going to give it my best efforts and really learn from it." He found the first meeting "a little overwhelming, because I was marking students who had excelled in school—and I didn't. I made it through, but I had to study hard. But I looked at it as an opportunity to give students an opportunity to excel at something I didn't excel at—and it helps me feel the pulse of what the youth are doing.

"When you read some of these scholarship applications, when you see what some of these students have done, you're amazed. Being exposed to high-achieving students, with all that open-mindedness and optimism and youthfulness and energy—that keeps you on your toes."

An assessor's work was spread over four months, from December into March or April, and Peter reckoned it took about fifty hours in total. What was that worth to the Foundation?

If the average assessor's time is valued at $100 an hour—and some, like Peter, would have much higher rates—then each assessor contributed about $5,000 in time that would otherwise have had to be paid for. Two hundred and fifty assessors at $5,000 means that the assessors were effectively giving at least $1.25 million to the students, or $12.5 million over the life of the Foundation—enough to pay for more than three thousand scholarships at $4,000 each.

In Peter Wong's world, this would be called leverage.

After four years, Peter became a paid "administrator"— essentially a chairman overseeing the work of six other assessors while still doing voluntary assessments himself.

"Administrators had an annual training session in Montreal, so you got to meet the people in the organization—great people like Stéphane and Melissa—and in the last four years the training sessions turned into a wonderful trip for my wife and me to get to know Montreal better, and get to know the Foundation better as well. That was very rewarding.

"Another rewarding thing was doing the interviews, meeting the students, and then later telling them that they've won. You got to do that as an administrator; that was the gold at the end of the rainbow when you got to make those telephone calls. That made it all worthwhile. I got to make about ten to twelve phone calls like that, usually in April. I tried to catch them before they left to go to school.

"You got every type of reaction you can imagine. Some of them were kind of expecting your call, and when you'd tell them they'd won a Provincial Award the were disappointed that they didn't get a National Award." He laughs. "I think that just happened once. But then you got other students breaking into tears on the telephone line, and you could hear their parents in the background doing cartwheels as well."

Was it all worthwhile?

"Oh, yes. If I didn't enjoy it, I wouldn't have done it—and it's the people from the organization that kept me involved as long as I was. I think I got back one hundred times more than what I gave to this organization."

Over the years, certain assessors became legendary within the program, among them Wayne Ludlow in Newfoundland, Sylvie Rossignol in Quebec, and Simon Cheng and Harold Lass in Toronto.

"Harold Lass was there since day one," says Stéphane Le-Blanc. "He was a joy to work with. He's a retired teacher so he knows the sector incredibly well. He was an administrator, an assessor, a renewal committee member, an In-course committee member—he did everything that we had people do. Whether it was paid or not paid, he was always there. Vesna Antwan was a new staff member in 2009, and the first time she worked with Harold, she sent me an email saying, 'This man is a machine, he's incredible!'"

"Harold is a fantastic person," Vesna nods. "He had written a book about Holocaust education and he had just done a big trek in the Himalayas. He's really amazing. You know, I think the administrators were really like our laureates—just really good, good people, very committed—and because a lot of them had been teachers themselves, I think that questions of access to post-secondary education were already in the forefront of their minds."

The volunteers, says Stéphane, were all deeply committed and truly understood what the program was trying to accomplish—particularly the administrators, who became very influential advisers to the Foundation staff. Yes, administrators did get an honorarium, but it was "far from being equivalent to the actual work that they did." He tells a story about Marie Verdun in southwestern Ontario, a very dedicated administrator.

"She accepted the job one year," says Stéphane, "and she said, 'But I'm pregnant and I should be giving birth right about at the end of the process.' She ended up giving birth to twins just before her interviews. Of course I sent her an email and congratulated her, and I said, 'Send us all the stuff, we'll finish the process.' She wouldn't do it. Not only did she finish the interviews, she prepared the lists of the winners and finished the whole thing. I was blown away, and she said, 'I love this; this is my favorite part of the process. I want to talk to these people. I want to make sure that we picked the right ones.' That kind of commitment blew me away."

That kind of commitment would often spring from the volunteers' growing appreciation of the quality of the young people whose lives they were changing. As one assessor remarked, going through the applications every year and learning what the young people were up to was "my antidote to cynicism."

THE ORIGINAL Excellence Award Program was essentially a university entrance award—like the vast majority of scholarships in Canada. But it soon became apparent that entrance programs were missing another very large group of deserving students, says Melissa Moi, who, after five years with the Foundation, was only twenty-seven when it closed. At a conference of students, she could easily have been taken for an undergraduate.

She and her colleagues developed the In-course Award Program "for students who are mid-way through their post-secondary studies—after their first year in college or their second year in university—and who have never previously been recognized by a merit scholarship. This is a segment of the population that maybe didn't have a 90 per cent average in high school, and maybe didn't do all the stuff that our entrance-award students were doing, but really hit their stride when they got into college and university."

The In-course scholarships, which Melissa administered, were awarded in partnership with over 230 institutions. Each institution had a specific number of nominations based on its school population. Many of the scholarships thus went to students at colleges, which traditionally didn't award many merit scholarships, and whose students weren't generally eligible for entrance scholarships from external sources.

"One result of the In-course program is that we picked up a ton of mature students, people who decided that they wanted to return to school later in life," Melissa says. "That's actually my soft spot—the mature student in the In-course awards. It's not the stereotype, the seventeen-year-old with the iPod. Some of these people were grandparents with beautiful stories. We had first-generation immigrants, people from rural communities in Newfoundland, from the North, from downtown Toronto, from Moose Jaw, from the Downtown Eastside in Vancouver. It was a broad view of Canadians as a people who are learning."

The In-course Award Program was comparable in size to the entrance program, and as its manager Melissa dealt with a range of administrative issues: assessment, renewals, database management and so forth. She also fielded questions from the recipients, and—like her colleagues on the Excellence Awards team—she often found herself serving as a resource far beyond her administrative responsibilities.

"We did ask questions, we did check in with them," she says. "I really enjoyed that part of my job. We wanted them to succeed, and we were here to support them if they were having problems. We knew that people are people, and things change, and stuff happens to them.

"So a lot of students ended up having a relationship with the Foundation where they talked to us about what was going on in their lives, if they were having problems with their health, with their school, with their families. These people were extremely involved in their communities, extremely involved in their schools, and there was a lot of pressure on many of them," Melissa explains. "A lot of them had burn-out, and they didn't feel comfortable enough to show their vulnerable side to anybody.

"Well, the irony of it is, why would you show that to a scholarship foundation that rewards you specifically on your achievement? But in some cases we were able to make those relationships happen. When the students were comfortable enough with us, they would call us on a regular basis." She laughs. "Someone told me they thought of me as this old woman pushing papers around on my desk. Then they met me and went 'Oh, my god! You're not old!'"

Annie Szulzyngier, who worked with Melissa, also treasured the relationships that could occur with students.

"Once the students were selected, we were like resource persons for them," she says. "So we followed them for the number of years they spent with us with their award." Like Melissa, she's delighted with "the energy that they put into their involvement, the fact that they could be so young and yet so powerful in what they were doing. They just had so much charisma that they really brought other people with them."

If it seems surprising that Foundation staff should have developed such a strong personal relationship with students, that fact also reveals something important about the way the educational system normally treats its most gifted participants. Unlike most entrance awards, about one-third of the

Millennium scholarships were renewable, as were one-third of the In-course Awards, and, says one former student leader, people at the Foundation were unusual in that they wanted their recipients to succeed, wanted to approve their renewals and worked very hard to help laureates through the inevitable rough patches. Institutions, he says, "don't do that. They give you an entrance scholarship and they want you to lose it—because their scholarships are as much about recruitment as recognition, and if you lose your scholarship, then the institution can use that money to recruit somebody else."

By contrast, says Andrew Woodall, Foundation staff were generally very mindful of the fact that they were dealing with people's lives, and they listened and learned and changed many aspects of what they did. They knew that "there were repercussions to our decisions. For example, if we had to terminate a laureate, we knew that it meant a lot to that person, so we had to be damn sure that we were doing the right thing. We had to be solid in our rationale and reasoning. We had to play through whether this was helping us or not, whether it was helping the student or not, and then make decisions that were based on equity, bearing in mind that it was a merit scholarship.

"It was much easier for us in the later years to do deferrals for psychological reasons as opposed to just physical illness, for instance. We also could do deferrals for economic reasons, which we never would have done in the early days. If someone couldn't pay for their education and they said that they needed to take some time out to make some cash, we let them do that."

Annie Szulzyngier believes that the Foundation's programs reshaped the way that some institutions view merit. In the academic world, merit is usually judged on the basis of marks—but marks in isolation actually mean very little. People can get good marks because they study very hard, or because they have a narrow gift. Working with the Foundation, however, led some institutions to reflect that merit should indeed include leadership, strength of character, innovativeness and citizenship. In the end, that reflection led them to consider those qualities even when they were bestowing other awards that had nothing to do with the Foundation.

"IN THE Excellence Awards Program, we said that the award was more than just a cheque," says Chad Lubelsky. "I worked on the 'more than just a cheque' part: the leadership development programs. The Excellence Awards were meant to recognize, encourage and support the students. The support was financial, the recognition was, 'congratulations, you won an award' and then the encouragement was what I did. The ancillary programs. The fun part."

The fun part involved two semi-annual Think Again national conferences, which brought together laureates from across the country for stimulating weekends in Ottawa and Toronto, and six annual conferences in regions across the country. It also included the online community called LaureateSpace.ca, as well as the operation of twenty-five local or institutional chapters; two meetings annually of chapter coordinators; a Millennium Grant Program that provided $2,500 top-up grants to support laureates while they did summer projects with Canadian non-governmental organizations; and a national network of Millennium alumni.

All of which means that Chad Lubelsky had perhaps a more intense and continuous engagement with the laureates than anyone else in the Foundation had. In a way, he represented the Foundation to the laureates and the laureates to the Foundation. Positioned at this borderline, he saw "a kind of reciprocity. The

Foundation transformed the students, yes, but the students also transformed the Foundation."

Stocky, balding, cheerful and enthusiastic, Chad was almost a legend within the little world of the Millennium Foundation.

Voices in the air:

Chad is a rock star with the laureates—as is Andrew.
He is superhuman in his dedication.
Chad is like a cult figure around here.
He's very jolly. He's permanently jolly. It's easy to feel comfortable around him.

· All true. At any meeting of laureates—at breakfast, during breaks, at dinner—young people clustered around Chad. Great gusts of laughter would sweep out from his table and wash over the rest of the room. People at other tables would look at each other and smile. "Chad," someone would grin, with a shake of the head.

Working at the Foundation was "a wonderful experience," Chad declares. "It's rare to see a group of people who are excited about things and willing to expose themselves a bit. Where I worked before was more of a cynical environment—but there was something very magical at the Foundation that enabled us to innovate. It was a function of who we worked with, and our capacity to absorb risk, to try things and take chances—like on a regional meeting, for instance. We could say, 'we're going to organize two conferences within a month'—and we'd be able to do that both in terms of resources and the trust between ourselves and the students that allowed us to take risks."

The event that Chad is remembering is the genesis of the six regional conferences. It came about in September 2005, when he and Andrew realized that the great power of the ancillary programs was that they brought people together—but they provided that benefit mainly to a small group of laureates at a national level. Could the Foundation do something to extend the reach of that benefit?

"The wonderful thing about working for an organization that has a short lifespan is that you don't want to waste a year," Chad observes. "So we decided—very, very quickly—to try to host regional conferences within a month. We called up John Centofanti, the chapter coordinator in Hamilton, and we said, 'Can you do this? Can you put together a conference, which will just be one night, in a month? And we'll send out the invites?' John jumped at it, and we did it, and we did the same thing in Halifax."

The result was a program of six regional meetings that were subsequently held annually right across the country, supplementing the meetings of the twenty-five local chapters and the semi-annual Think Again conferences. What happened, says Andrew Woodall, is that a chapter would decide that it wanted to host a regional conference, and its members would talk to other chapters within their region about the date and the content of the conference. They might invite speakers or Millennium alumni, or they might just use their own members to provide workshops and presentations. The Foundation would help them arrange travel, book a venue and order food. And the Foundation paid for it all.

"The joke of it," says Andrew, "is that when we got there we had no idea what was about to happen. We generally knew who was supposed to be there because we had lists of people. We knew when the meals were going to be served and what they were going to be. If we were lucky, we'd have an outline of what was supposed to happen, but sometimes we didn't.

"So we got there and it was this great chaotic sort of process that was going on and we just rolled with it. Those meetings were much mellower than our national conferences. The primary goal was for the laureates to get to know each other. As a result, we saw chapter activity go up, for instance. People went to a regional meeting, and they'd say, 'Oh there's chapters? I didn't know that. Wow, there's one on my campus.' We got people using regional meetings to come up with ideas for the Millennium Grants, the $2,500 top-up. It became a really important aspect of the ancillary program, at least equal to all the others. If we look at the objective of supporting the developing of the network of students to make Canada a better place, the regional meetings became a huge link."

Chad notes that the regional meetings provided "a real leadership development opportunity for the students who were involved in the organizing. And through the regional meetings we were able to invite every single national and provincial laureate in the country. They then had much more of a connection to the network, and they were much more likely to become involved." By broadening the opportunities for students to connect with "the fun part" of the program, the regional meetings strengthened the reciprocal relationship between the students and the Foundation, and thus transformed the program itself.

That transformation was visible even in the regional meetings themselves. The first year, Chad had sleepless nights before each of the meetings because he had been responsible for sinking a fair amount of money into the events, and he had no idea what they were going to be like. The students were equally nervous, uncertain about their mission and unclear about the limits of their autonomy. What decisions could they make by themselves? Could they buy pens? Could they afford speakers?

Chad and Andrew soon learned that the laureates could do an excellent job of creating the content for the meetings, and that the Foundation could hand over a great deal of administrative control to them as well. In the end, the Foundation simply told the organizers that they had a budget of so many dollars per student to spend as they saw fit. The Foundation took care of food, meeting rooms and travel; the rest was up to the laureates.

"We learned that things didn't always have to be organized the way we expected them to be organized," says Chad. "There's a lot of different ways of getting from A to Z. We didn't necessarily even need to know what was going on. Sometimes we didn't know all the laureates who were involved. And the conferences were always surprising and always really different, which surprised us. What happened in Fredericton was very different from what happened out west, let alone Toronto. They were all flavoured with their regions."

The same regional flavouring characterized the chapters, which Chad believes were the most important ancillary program of all.

"We learned that place is very important in Canada," he says, "and that people identify much more with being from Saskatoon, for example, than being Canadian. That's not to say that being Canadian isn't important, but Saskatoon is very important too. There was a national raison d'être for the chapters, but how that raison d'être manifested itself locally was different from place to place. And so the chapters were the places where I think there was the most learning for us, the places where we got to know the students the best, and so for us that's where there was the deepest learning about who these people were."

The Foundation brought the chapter coordinators together three times a year, a pattern created at the suggestion of the coordinators themselves.

"The chapters were where the values of the program were moulded, at least for me," says Chad. "And in many, many places on a local level, the chapters didn't need the Foundation, which

I think was a huge success. The laureates in London, Ontario, or in Saskatoon or in Halifax are going to stay connected to each other. We did our job. Connecting those laureates in Halifax to Edmonton and creating a national network? There's still work to be done there."

THE CONSTRUCTION of a national network of young leaders was a conscious goal of the Excellence Awards Program. Canada is a highly regionalized country, and its pan-Canadian institutions—the railways, the CBC, the social programs—have been steadily weakened over the last few decades. The Millennium network strongly asserted values and connections that are national rather than regional.

"We were all about positive change, about growth," says Norman Riddell. "So whether it was the employees or the clients or anyone else, it was always about changing people in a positive direction. Not everyone approved. We've been called arrogant, and I've been told that it sounded like social engineering. A good friend of mine, a very high-powered consultant, called my approach to the Excellence Awards 'Stalinist.'

"But you know, our approach was, I am not trying to tell you what you're going to be. I am going to expose you to things that you may not have thought about before. And I'm going to ask you to suspend judgement and try to empathize with other people so you can understand. You don't have to agree with it, just understand where they're coming from."

The Foundation's first initiative to draw its laureates together was the Think Again conferences, which began in 2000. The September conference, in Ottawa, brought together all National Award holders, both new and renewed. The January conference, in Toronto, was dedicated specifically to the newly appointed laureates.

Think Again was much more highly organized and showy, much more structured, than the student-led regional meetings. In September 2008, for instance, laureates from across the country gathered in the Government Conference Centre—the refurbished Ottawa railway station—for two and a half days of listening and talking, reflecting and absorbing, thinking and linking. The networking objective was explicit; Norman Riddell's welcome in the conference booklet noted that "we are working diligently to make sure that all the connections you have made amongst yourselves over the past years are not lost and that this conference is a focal point of this network building activity." Each delegate's kit included a batch of personalized business cards bearing the delegate's phone number and email address, and the laureates were encouraged to exchange them freely.

Earlier Think Again conferences had heard speakers like author Joy Kogawa, then–Governor General Adrienne Clarkson, and Denise Donlon, former president of Sony Canada. Another speaker was Roch Carrier, the award-winning novelist, former director of the Canada Council, former national librarian of Canada and former playwright-in-residence at the Théâtre du Nouveau Monde. Carrier is also the author of the beloved short story "The Hockey Sweater," a snippet from which appears on the Canadian five-dollar bill. People still chuckle at the memory of Carrier, surrounded by laureates, inscribing his autograph on five-dollar bills.

The 2008 plenary sessions included Jeffrey Kluger expounding upon "simplexity," the topic of his most recent book, and Meg Wheatley of the Berkana Institute talking about ways to conduct the strenuous work of leadership for social change without collapsing into burn-out. The essence of the matter was relationships, "the building blocks of life. We are all bundles of potential that manifest only in relationships." A leader, she said, is "anyone willing to help—so the world is full of change agents." She summarized her message in the Zulu concept of "ubuntu," meaning "we can be human only together."

In breakout sessions, laureates discussed global citizenship, new media, program planning and design, The Natural Step organization, electronic volunteerism, the triple bottom line in business, interpersonal skills. One such session was devoted to "managing the screens of your life"—the multiple identities that flow from participating in social media such as Facebook, MySpace, LinkedIn, Tumblr, Twitter, Digg and so on. The leader of the session was a stubble-bearded social-networking oracle named Eli Singer who vigorously tackled some tricky and puzzling aspects of social media. For instance, why do people want to tell the world that they were blind drunk or hopelessly stoned last night? Why would you post your photo albums, your videos, your opinions about art and politics and religion, your cell phone number and the directions for guests to get to your house party?

An astute McGill undergraduate named Johnson Fung had some interesting observations. In earlier periods, he said, people found their identities in relationships with family, community, church, profession and other social groups. In a fluid postmodern world, the importance of those groupings has faded, and the roots of identity have become mysterious. Facebook and its ilk allow people to forge and shape their identities as an act of will, with reference to a community of electronic peers.

Cool. But Eli Singer, a hoary old relic of thirty-one, proved to be an advocate of caution. He reminded the group that recruiters and employers routinely check out a potential employee's Facebook page and silently reject stoners and party animals. A student remarked that elite graduate schools do the same thing.

Eli recounted the tale of the Saugeen Stripper who, in a moment of lighthearted lunacy, peeled for the boys in a University of Western Ontario residence while the cameras were rolling. The footage became one of the most-watched videos in cyberspace, and though the girl had done nothing illegal, the publicity forced her to leave school.

"Control your information," Eli counselled. "You have to manage the screens of your life, the way you present yourself online." Remember, he said, Facebook forgets nothing. Google forgets nothing—it keeps copies of every single email. Own your own domain. Blog on your own site. Turn your Facebook privacy settings up to the max. If you don't want something known, don't release it. In the cyber world there's really no escape. There's even a social networking site for the dead, where your estate can post your social-networking information. It's called Footnote.com. Electronic immortality. Who knew?

A high point of Think Again was a dinner at the Canadian War Museum, with the tables set among the tanks and fighter planes and Bren gun carriers. The dinner concluded with a performing arts presentation such as a structured improvisation by the Four Chambers Dance Project. On one memorable occasion, a laureate named Patrick Yann, who studied opera, offered to sing. Norman Riddell received the suggestion with enthusiasm— and offered to accompany Patrick on the piano.

The Foundation rented a piano. The CEO played it. The student sang. The performance was splendid, and the crowd was delighted.

THINK AGAIN was the fountainhead of the ancillary programs; it was the first, and the later programs grew out of the excellence team's experience with it. The chapters grew out of Think Again, and so did the online community LaureateSpace.ca, which may eventually prove the most durable networking legacy of the Foundation.

When the Foundation undertook its mid-term consultations with its stakeholders, the excellence team convened a meeting in Toronto, an "exploration session," to which a number of people involved in youth engagement had been invited. One of the ideas that emerged from the session was the notion that if the laureates could be given a little bit of project money, they would probably do some very valuable things. The eventual result was a proposal for what became the Millennium Grant Program (MGP).

"Now the MGP is a great example of how our programs changed," says Chad Lubelsky. The first year, the program criteria were very rigid. "Only graduating students were allowed to do it. Nothing abroad. Maximum one hundred students. One deadline. And the take-up in the end was disappointing.

"We went away and scratched our heads a little bit, and when we talked to students we found out that they were intimidated by the program, and that the one deadline didn't work, and that some of the conditions were a little bit too restrictive. And we weren't very happy with the quality of the applications, either. Also, it wasn't going to be competitive, because we had enough of a budget that we could give grants out to everybody who applied.

"So over the course of the following year, we changed it and changed it and changed it again. Eventually the MGP application became an interactive process. The students applied, three alumni assessed the applications and wrote comments, and then we fed the comments back to the students. The whole point of the program was what were you going to learn, and how were you going to know that you'd learned it? It was about providing opportunities to act and opportunities to reflect, both right in the loop. So that's what they had to talk about." The staff worked with the applicants to develop the plan until it met the program's requirements.

Julie Danielse, who later worked with Chad on MGP, saw additional opportunities for improvement. She initiated pre-project meetings, bringing laureates in the same vicinity together before their individual projects began. Sensing a need for project monitoring, she visited projects whenever she could. When she travelled to cities like Montreal, Ottawa, Toronto, Vancouver and St. John's, she invited laureates to join her for an "MGP get-together" over lunch or coffee, comparing experiences, swapping ideas and socializing.

Julie also set up a program on LaureateSpace.ca called "MGP Coaches," where any interested laureate could ask the advice of experienced MGP recipients. And, because she wanted to see some of the overseas projects in action, she vacationed in Peru and Costa Rica at her own expense and went to visit MGP projects while she was there.

Among her favourite stories, she says, are the ones you rarely heard about, "when laureates continued their MGP projects after the MGP was finished. At that point they weren't usually getting paid any longer, but they continued to work out of pure passion." She's also very moved by stories from laureates who came home from working in developing countries "with a completely different view of themselves and international work"—an experience she had herself after volunteering in Tanzania in 2007.

FOR AN outside observer, the line between the laureates and the excellence team becomes blurred over time. The two groups are cut from the same swatch of cloth. The staff might well have been laureates themselves if the program had existed in their day.

"We were a weird two-way inward-outward mirror," says Andrew Woodall. "We got a lot out of the laureates and we reflected a lot back on them, but it also reflected back on us when we saw them do things. Maybe it was like the mirrors in the barber shop, you know, where it could go on forever, reflecting back and forth."

In fact, many of the staff were also students themselves, having taken advantage of the Foundation's educational support program for employees. The Foundation was, says Norman Riddell, "a learning organization, so we did some unusual things. Anybody on our staff who wanted to undertake further study could do it. I paid $25,000 to $30,000 for people to study to get particular diplomas. Anything they wanted to do, we would pay for—provided they succeeded. I didn't pay for failures."

Melissa Moi, for instance, completed an MA at Concordia University while working full-time at the Foundation. She had always known that if she wanted to continue her education, the Foundation would support her, and she made the decision to study while she was working "so that I could give back to the Foundation what they were giving to me. And also, adult learning principles say that you need to apply what you learn in theory, so I chose a program where I'd go to class, and then I'd go to work the next day, and I would see the learning that I'd had in my class come out at work. So I could change the way that I was doing things based on what I'd actually learned in class."

For similar reasons, Chad Lubelsky enrolled in an MA program at Royal Roads University in Victoria.

"Education was a big value at the Foundation," he says, "and I'd get frustrated with my job sometimes, feeling that I was doing things—and spending a lot of money sometimes—based on instinct. I didn't feel comfortable doing that. I wanted to feel that this instinct was based more on a solid footing. So I thought that I had a responsibility to train myself a little bit more, to make sure that I could back what I was doing."

Other staff took courses in computer operations, in languages, in journalism. And, says Andrew Woodall, not all the learning took place in institutions. The workplace itself was an educational venue.

Melissa Moi, Annie Szulzyngier and Stéphane LeBlanc, for instance, researched the overall state of merit scholarships in Canada—a project that came out of conversations among them about the trends they were seeing in their daily work. To gather the data, Melissa made a lightning foray across the country, talking to Foundation contacts and convening meetings of interested parties. Where else, she asks, would she have been allowed simply to "take the time off from my day-to-day job to go and do this, just because this was really important to us?"

Another example is the online application and renewal process, which Melissa also spearheaded. This is the twenty-first century, after all, and everything from shopping to sex to spirituality is online—and students expected to be able to file their applications online. Melissa saw the need, discussed it with her colleagues, got together with a contractor and saw the project through. It made the Foundation a leader in the field.

"We presented at conferences," says Melissa. "People consulted with us. We went down to the States to a National Scholarship Providers Association conference, where we presented what we'd done, and we learned that a major computer company had done the same thing—but it cost them hundreds of thousands to do it, plus three years of development. We did it in a year and a half with just me, a contractor and a programmer.

"We always had an eye to contributing to the work of the larger community. We always were very open and consultative, telling others what we were doing, saying 'If you need the technology, let us know. What's ours is yours.' Now some universities are interested in using it, and some provincial agencies have been looking at it as a basis for province-wide applications. It's been really cool."

"MERIT SCHOLARSHIPS, if done well, are not just about supporting people to keep doing what they're doing," declares Franca Gucciardi, who is now back as executive director at the Canadian Merit Scholarship Foundation, the same organization that once awarded a scholarship to her. "They're about encouraging them and inspiring them to live up to the fullest expression of their potential, which is something that a country really needs to invest in. Because that kind of achievement doesn't just happen magically. It happens because opportunities are provided to make sure that the potential is fully realized.

"As Canadians, this is one of the things we just have to do better. We have to understand that talent needs to be nurtured, that opportunity needs to be provided, that we can't be afraid of innovation, that we need to invest resources in those things.

"People tell me all the time, 'Oh, people like that will be fine without you.' But it's not okay for gifted people just to be fine. I don't want them to be *fine*. I want them to be *great!*"

› An Orphanage in Nepal

. . . .

OLIN MACDONALD's trip to Kathmandu started with a conversation at a breakfast table in Montreal. His friend Mishuka Adikary was contemplating volunteer service in Nepal with an organization called Volunteer Abroad. Colin didn't know where Nepal was, but he was captivated by the idea.

Mishuka—"Mish," as she's known—certainly did know where Nepal was. She was born in Bangladesh and raised in Taiwan and Toronto. A pre-med student at the University of Western Ontario, she could speak and write English, Bengali and Mandarin. She named her interests as "drawing, dancing, learning new stuff (I wish I had a personal plane), helping the community, air hockey, movies, hearing babies laugh and watching LIVE football games." She said that eventually she hoped to join Doctors without Borders.

Mish had dreamed of doing something in Asia for children. As a laureate, she was eligible for a Millennium Project Grant to work with a Canadian non-profit organization. She immediately approached Volunteer Abroad. Could she do her summer work overseas? Maybe in Asia? In, say, Nepal?

Colin comes from Charlottetown, Prince Edward Island. As a teen, he had volunteered at the hospital, the Humane Society and Big Brothers Big Sisters, as well as directing a youth theatre. He had been involved with Junior Achievement and had done presentation workshops and marketing projects with Advancing Canadian Entrepreneurship. A French immersion student himself, he had worked with Canadian Parents for French and had been a counsellor at a French-language summer camp.

With all this volunteering, his friends thought he was crazy. Even his parents thought he overworked. When he got the phone call from the Foundation telling him he had won an Excellence Award, "I remember hanging up the phone in disbelief. I was home alone, and I started crying, and then I immediately called everyone that I thought would care, because it was the greatest gift someone could ask for—being recognized for your community work, the recognition that you've done good."

Not surprisingly, both he and Mish soon emerged as chapter coordinators, organizing events for the laureates in their regions and participating in national conferences and workshops. In January 2007, they were both attending a coordinators' meeting in Montreal. Over breakfast, Mish mentioned the Nepal idea to her friend Natalie Poole, from Saskatchewan. Natalie instantly offered to go along, as did four other students at the table, including Colin Macdonald.

The group grew to eleven students from all across Canada. Mish set up a Facebook page so that everyone could participate equally in the planning. When they presented themselves to Volunteer Abroad, the organization looked for a project that could utilize the whole group. It chose the Grace Home/St. Grace School, a non-profit organization in Kathmandu that provides a home and an education to vulnerable and orphaned children. The Grace Home also takes in disabled and destitute elders who can learn skills and help with child care in return for food and lodging.

During a five-week stay, what could eleven Canadian students do for an orphanage in Kathmandu? Quite a bit, as it turned out.

"It's an orphanage and a school for about fourteen children who live there, and an additional six to ten from low-income families who just attend school there," Colin explains, sitting in a coffee shop in Halifax, where he studies education at Mount Saint Vincent University. The Grace Home, he says, was little more than "four brick walls and half a roof, almost like a compound, and the ground was covered in broken bricks.

"We lifted up all those broken bricks and laid new bricks and painted all the walls. We added a classroom with a roof, which provided a place where the children could distinguish home life from school life. Before we did this, the children were being taught in their bedrooms because there just wasn't anywhere else."

The Canadian students built playground equipment—swings and slides—and redecorated all the bedrooms. Because the school's water supply produced rusty water, the Grace Home had been forced to buy expensive drinking water. The Canadians passed the hat among themselves, raised a little money and erected a small water tower with a proper filtration system. They also started a composting system and a small organic garden in the schoolyard. Mish made a video about the project, and posted it on YouTube.

Nepali tradesmen don't normally work much during the rainy season, but the Canadians only had a few weeks, so they stretched tarps over the work sites and kept on working, which made a real impact on the neighbours. Before the project, says

Mish, local people hadn't paid much attention to the orphanage, "but now, here were all these volunteers working in the rain to help these kids," which greatly raised the profile of the orphanage within its own community.

"I was interested in education, but I wasn't sure if it was really for me," Colin reflects. "Well, while we were there, I was able to teach throughout the mornings at the school. I have a theatre background, so I got the children learning English through theatre. We did health and medical checkups, nutrition, health and hygiene—how to wash your hands, how to brush your teeth, things like that." They also enlisted local doctors, and started a proper system of medical and dental records.

This was the first group of Millennium students to use their Millennium Project Grants to volunteer overseas. The next year, a second group of Millennium students continued the work at the Grace Home. In later years, students worked on MGP grants in Nicaragua, Senegal, Benin, El Salvador, Ecuador, Peru, Kenya, Liberia and Sri Lanka—and also in every corner of Canada.

Looking back, Colin Macdonald believes that the Nepali kids got a lot out of the project, "but I got a lot more out of it. And there's not a day goes by that I don't think about the school, and the children and that amazing country."

> *five*

REDEFINING ACCESS

. . . .

"RESEARCH WAS not part of the original concept of the Foundation," says Andrew Parkin, munching on a clubhouse sandwich in
his corner office, squeezing in a conversation in the only time
slot available. He was the Foundation's associate executive director, Norman Riddell's second-in-command, and he also headed
its eight-person research team. A tall, rangy, sandy-haired man,
he's perfectly at home in the arcane crannies of social science
research and also perfectly comfortable explaining them. The
need for research turned out to be inherent in the way the Foundation's mission was set forth, he observes, and the results will
constitute an important part of the organization's legacy.

The research program began with a review of what was actually known about student aid in Canada. The answer: not much.

"Our job in the first instance really was to understand what
we were doing, and the environment in which we were operating," Parkin continues. "Who were the students? What was the

student profile? What kinds of obstacles did they face? How were they actually paying for school? How much were governments actually spending on student aid?"

Basic information. Surely such things were perfectly well known? Well, no.

"For example, Canada Student Loans publishes a report every year about how many loans they issue and how much money students are borrowing," Parkin explains. "And you think, well, that's a really good thing to know. Then you pick up the report, and the numbers seem low. Well, that's because Canada Student Loans provides only 60 per cent of a student's loan. The other 40 per cent comes from the province. And no one puts out a report on what students are borrowing overall or how many loan dollars are out there overall.

"The original research program, when Alex Usher started it, was just filling in the blanks, but that's where you got some of the key insights that the Foundation learned during this period. We learned that there are many barriers that students face. Some of them are financial, but they're not all financial. Governments are spending a lot of money to help students, but not all of it is spent in the most effective ways.

"Since then we added two more dimensions. One of them was more formal program evaluation. Were our programs working? What evidence was there of our impact? The second, and by far the most unique, was the pilot projects, which were designed to test different hypotheses about what could be done to improve access."

Voices in the air:

Andrew Parkin is a brilliant academic.
Andrew Parkin is a genius.

He runs a very efficient operation. All the research is contracted to others. It's just developed and guided by Andrew and his people.

He has a really good handle on methodology, which just makes my eyes glaze over.

He hides it, but Andrew's got this real kind of rogue lefty thing about social equity and social justice. He wants to get at these deeper questions about who's missing and who's being left out.

It drives Andrew bananas when some government has a program and they're claiming it works—and they have no evidence to actually support that.

THE FOUNDATION was established at the end of a decade of rising tuition and sharply increased student debt, and in the realization that while 80 per cent of the new jobs that were being created in Canada required some form of post-secondary education, only 67 per cent of school leavers were choosing to continue their studies. Young people, it seemed, were looking at the cost of higher education and simply declining to pay it, and the result was a growing mismatch between the labour force and the labour market. By reducing the cost of higher education, the Foundation's bursaries would presumably induce more young people to undertake further studies, which would help to narrow the gap between what the economy needed and what the labour force could provide.

On that understanding—which was the basis of its mandate— the Foundation set up its operations and established its programs. But was that understanding accurate? Would scholarships and bursaries in themselves increase access? What was access anyway? In order to determine that you had improved it, you would need somehow to measure it, and also to measure changes in it—as well as showing that positive changes were a result of the

Foundation's activities. In short, to determine whether you were achieving your purpose, you would have to do research—and rather sophisticated research at that.

"There was a very definite feeling within the Board of Directors that they had not been given nearly enough information," recalls Alex Usher, the Foundation's first research director. "They felt that they had made decisions on the disposal of the $300 million a year far too quickly, and with far too little information. I heard later that one of them—possibly Monty—had said that one of the best presents we could make to the nation would be knowledge, so that the next time someone was given $2.5 billion, they'd have a better idea of how to spend it."

For Norman Riddell, the research program was also an essential aspect of the Foundation's accountability.

"Our thinking changed because we did research in our program," Riddell explained much later. "If we discovered it wasn't working, we made adjustments. If we found even those didn't work, then we tried something else.

"All of this was in support of an idea that we hope will eventually get implanted in Canada. Public money is not money that is given voluntarily. It is provided in the form of taxes, and no taxpayer wants to turn a lot of money over to the government. Public money should be used very carefully, and it should be used for maximum impact.

"So, rather than just taking a bright idea and throwing a huge amount of money at it, isn't it better to experiment to find out what kind of effect it will have before putting the program in place? We have lots and lots of bad examples. The Canada Student Loans Program is a perfect example. It's a huge program, and billions of dollars have been spent, but no one has any idea what has changed. We have some nice anecdotes, but for a few billion dollars you should know more than that. And even when Ottawa put its new program into place, the program that will succeed the Foundation, they didn't include a provision for evaluation. There's still no appetite in Ottawa for putting an evaluation framework around the things that they do in order to find out what the impact is."

A lack of rigorous program evaluation results in government guesswork—designing and launching programs designed to combat unemployment, encourage innovation, improve public health or whatever, without knowing or learning what works and what doesn't. Perhaps the officials who devise and implement such programs don't really want to know their impact. In today's deeply partisan atmosphere, there would often be a political penalty for failure, and there might not be much of a political reward for success.

An independent agency like a foundation, by contrast, is only indirectly answerable to masters in the political arena, and it is much more mission-focused than most public agencies. It can afford to consider the longer term, review its activities, recognize its mistakes and change course without being condemned in Parliament for its imperfections. And, notes Parkin, because the Foundation had only one area of responsibility, its board—unlike a government—was not deflected by a continuing series of crises and concerns in various areas. It didn't care about scandals, dilemmas or elections. It only cared about student aid, and it kept coming back to the staff demanding to know how the programs were working.

So program evaluation became a vitally important support to the Foundation's management. But the impact of a program can't be measured until the program has been operating for some time. The major example of evaluation was the

Queen's University mid-term report of 2003, which was required by the legislation, and which resulted in the whole new suite of provincial programs of Millennium Access Bursaries unveiled in 2005—which, unlike the original bursary programs, had provisions for evaluation built into their design.

Initially, however, the point of departure for the Millennium Research Program was to assemble a body of knowledge about access to post-secondary education, which is all about the behaviour of students and potential students. What determines access? What makes a young person—or, for that matter, an older person—decide to pursue further education? How are potential students affected by factors like their reading ability, the experiences of other family members, the outlook of their peers? Will they choose university, college, trade school, apprenticeship? In what field? In what location? With what goal? What considerations shape these decisions? And what role does money actually play?

The Foundation's very first research publication, in fact, was a short, unsigned paper entitled "Does Money Matter?" The paper noted that the research program had two basic functions. First, it aimed to support the mid-mandate evaluation process required by the Foundation's governing legislation. Second, it was intended to improve the Foundation's products and make them more useful to students.

130   The research program, the paper noted, was based in the legislation, which declared that the Foundation's purpose was "to improve access to post-secondary education by giving money to students in need." The obvious assumption was that money played a determining role in student decision making about higher education. Most people probably believed that. But was it true? Did money, in itself, really shape student choices, or

were other factors equally or more important? And if money did matter, exactly how did it matter? Did it matter equally to everyone? Would parents or students react differently to different "forms" of money such as loans, grants, tuition discounts and tax breaks?

"In the absence of adequate answers to these questions," said the paper, "it is impossible to evaluate the effect the Foundation has had and equally difficult to evaluate the merit of other possible program designs." Or, as Alex Usher puts it, "Some of us felt strongly that we had to be judged as a failure or a success based on how much difference *any* financial aid institution could have made."

In keeping with its philosophy of doing only the things that only it could do, the Foundation commissioned academics and other researchers to review the state of student finances, investigate the reasoning of young people who did not go on to higher education and describe the gaps in our knowledge of the factors that affect such choices. Even before that, it had forged links to the student aid community, the people who were dealing with student needs and decisions on a daily basis. In 2000, the Foundation's members held their first annual meeting in Calgary, and the Foundation invited the Canadian Association of Student Financial Aid Administrators (CASFAA) to assemble thirty-five or forty of its members for a discussion—at the Foundation's expense—of student aid policy.

The discussion became a wide-ranging tour of the whole topic of student financial aid in Canada, Alex Usher recalls, specifically "what do we do well, what do we not do so well, what could we do more—and out of that emerged a clear desire to know more."

Thus began a tradition of holding a CASFAA research and policy conference in conjunction with the Foundation's annual

131

meeting—and, indeed, of supporting the growth of CASFAA
itself. In the Foundation's early days, CASFAA was a small network loosely linking student aid professionals in different
universities and provinces, but once it became apparent how use-
fully the organization and the research program complemented
one another, the Foundation began funding an additional policy conference every June that ultimately brought together two
or three hundred professionals involved in student financial
assistance. The Foundation sponsored the conferences, and its
research team helped to delineate the issues and potential solutions and set the agenda.

"It wasn't my area, but I always went to these conferences,"
says Randolf Harrold, the head of the Foundation's bursary
program. "I was always pleased and impressed that we made
major contributions to policy development, to networking, to
the growth of professional abilities among the student financial
assistance community across the country.

"That community came together again in a research and policy conference every year in September in Ottawa, associated
with our annual general meeting," Harrold continues. "That's
also when we held Think Again, the national event for Excellence
Award winners. So there was a lot of cross-fertilization in the
student financial assistance community and in the educational
community as a whole. The event was attended by educators from
universities and from government, and international interests
were represented as well. We tied that into the OECD education
community, and in April 2008 we put together a major international conference in Toronto. I don't think there's any doubt that
the Foundation made a major contribution in that area."

The research program, says Norman Riddell, "allowed us to
exercise soft leadership." The conferences that the Foundation

132

sponsored really created the student aid community in Canada, says Kevin Chapman, the former Director of Nova Scotia's Student Assistance Office. "It actually demystified the whole subject. I could call somebody and say, Look, I remember you did a presentation on this in September. Can you send me something about that? So you have contacts, and you have a face to put to a name. It provides a whole network of folks that you can go to."

The Foundation was also unique, says Andrew Parkin, in that its research was designed to be used, and its research staff was encouraged to present papers at conferences and participate in discussions of their findings. Other researchers—in Statistics Canada, for instance, or even in the universities—don't always have that mandate.

"StatsCan has this great Youth in Transition survey that they created in 1999, and that's following two cohorts of youth, and surveying them every two years," Parkin says. "That's the type of research instrument that everyone wishes they had, waves of surveys, but it's incredibly expensive. So StatsCan does that, and they write reports, but they don't go to the various corners of the country to talk about it."

They don't? Well, Parkin explains, sometimes they do, but their presentations are frequently given to economists and other statisticians who are interested mainly in the methodology employed. It's relatively rare for them to present to groups who are really affected by their conclusions and in the implications for policy. So one thing that the Foundation's research team did was "to take all these reports and say, 'this is what the reports are telling us about what's going on in our sector.'"

After the initial CASFAA meeting in Calgary, Alex Usher and his colleague Sean Junor reviewed what was known about student finances and financial aid in Canada. In general, the state of knowledge about education in Canada was far from satisfactory, partly because there really is no such thing as "education in Canada." Education is constitutionally a provincial responsibility, and provincial educational systems are as distinct and separate as Balkan principalities. In some provinces, universities are governed by the Department of Education; in others they are the responsibility of a separate ministry that may be responsible for vocational education as well. Curricula, school size, language of instruction, teacher certification, university grants, educational statistics—nothing is consistent from one province to another. One stunning example: Nobody actually knows the exact number of college students in Canada because the statistics and definitions are not consistent from province to province.

Usher and Junor dug up everything they could find about student costs, sources of income, barriers to entry, financial assistance from governments and other sources, and so forth. They used data collected by organizations such as the Canadian Undergraduate Survey Consortium, Acumen Research, and—above all—Statistics Canada. They commissioned EKOS Research to conduct a monthly national survey of student income and expenditure during the 2001–02 school year. They pulled all the results together and published their findings in a two-hundred-page volume called *The Price of Knowledge: Access and Student Finance in Canada*.

The chapters in *The Price of Knowledge* were organized around topics such as student preparations for higher education, characteristics of the student body, student costs and resources, and assistance provided by governments and other sources. The penultimate chapter discussed graduate outcomes—the level of debt carried by graduates, their record of loan repayment, their transitions to the labour force and their earnings in employment.

The final chapter considered the social benefits of higher education, otherwise known as the "return on public investment." The data revealed that the 40 per cent of Canadians who are college and university graduates pay more than 60 per cent of personal income taxes and receive less than a third of government transfer payments to individuals. That sentence on its own is a powerful statement of the financial case for public investment in higher education. The authors summarized its importance by noting that the financial contribution of graduates to the treasury "is so large that it is difficult to imagine the continuance of a welfare state in Canada without it."

The publication had a remarkable impact.

"We released *The Price of Knowledge* on September 16, 2002, and we had no idea the impact that it was going to have," says Joey Berger, who was then on the communications staff. "Over the summer I remember sitting in the boardroom with maybe half the office trying to figure out, like, what are we going to do with this thing and how are people going to know about it? We did a press conference, hoping that somebody would pay attention. It was Yom Kippur, so I was off that day, and I remember getting text messages on my phone twenty minutes in advance that we were going live on Newsworld. I remember watching *The National* that night, and there was a fifteen-second clip with one of our charts—and there must have been dozens of articles in different papers across the country the next day."

The Price of Knowledge ultimately came out in four editions, in 2002, 2004 and 2007, with a final edition in 2009. It became required reading for everyone in the student aid field in Canada, says Nova Scotia's Kevin Chapman.

"It was incredibly valuable, particularly for smaller jurisdictions where we simply didn't have the capacity to do that kind of research on our own," he observes. "And it's hard to do credible research on your own programs, but the Foundation's research was always seen to be objective. So if we were going to go to Cabinet and seek public policy changes that involved budget, we used the Foundation's research to supplement or reinforce our case.

"They did some wonderful research, and they were very open to sharing it, very open to including anyone that wanted to be involved. So that provided smaller jurisdictions like Nova Scotia with an opportunity to participate, and if you ever had a research idea you could call the Foundation and talk it through, and often they would support it financially."

The partnership with the Foundation—and particularly the research findings—had a huge impact on student aid services in Nova Scotia, Chapman says.

"Ultimately, we created our policy section here in Nova Scotia," he says, "and I think to a large degree the reason we were able to do that was because of the value that the politicians saw in research as a result of the Foundation's work. We were able to hire a manager of policy and three policy officers, which is unheard of. Eventually we added seven or eight people.

"We developed an outreach program because the Foundation's research had shown the value of early intervention. We reduced the amount that parents had to contribute towards their children's post-secondary education. We put a program in place with the Foundation to provide an upfront access grant for students from low-income families and supplemented that with provincial money in years 2, 3 and 4. We implemented a new grant for everybody that got a Nova Scotia student loan by making the first 20 per cent of the loan non-repayable. We had a new grant that provided assistance to students with children.

"These were fairly significant initiatives, and very targeted at specific populations—and they were all based on the Foundation's research and then on the work of our own policy section."

THE RESEARCH effort, the conferences and the discussions about access eventually produced at least five insights that fundamentally reshaped the way the student aid community thinks about access.

First, despite the assumptions that underlie the Foundation's legislation, *giving money to students who are already in post-secondary education does not address the question of access,* except possibly by reassuring both high school and post-secondary students that they will be able to afford to continue. But the research suggests that the Foundation's huge program of bursaries did not have that impact on high school students because most students know almost nothing about how to finance post-secondary study.

The key point is that, by definition, anyone enrolled in post-secondary education has already achieved access. Questions about access therefore relate mainly to people who are not in the system.

Second, the level of a student's indebtedness does not accurately indicate the level of his or her need. Surprisingly, the researchers found that the highest levels of debt are often associated with relatively well-off students from middle-class families enrolled in expensive courses in universities beyond commuting distance from their homes, and who are not working. The students who are most in need come from poor homes and do everything possible to minimize costs. They live at home, attend nearby institutions, don't enroll in high-cost programs like medicine and law, and often work part-time or even full-time to support their studies. Furthermore, low-income students often have

137

almost an allergic reaction to debt. For middle-class families, debt is simply a tool. For low-income families, debt is a monster that can eat you alive.

Third, treating everyone equally does not treat everyone equally. Different situations—even different regions of residence—create different needs. Kevin Chapman noted that Ontario had introduced a program of assistance for students living more than sixty-five kilometres from a post-secondary institution. In Nova Scotia, he smiled, "we could bring in a program like that and never spend a cent." No Nova Scotian lives more than fifty kilometres from the sea; by the same token, with forty-four career colleges, eleven universities and thirteen branches of the Nova Scotia Community College scattered across a very small province, no Nova Scotian lives more than sixty-five kilometres from post-secondary education.

One size never fits all. In fact, Chapman notes, an ill-fitting solution may actually become a burden. Suppose that a student needs $20,000, but the system can only provide $10,000. Are we doing that person any favours by providing enough money to get started—but not enough to keep going? A student who can't complete the program and doesn't get the degree is left with nothing but the debt.

Fourth, access is a much more complex matter than anyone had realized. The obstacles to entry vary with class, income, ethnicity, region and culture, and they are also closely related to the qualities that allow people to persist in post-secondary education and complete their programs. (Persistence, of course, can be seen as a form of access.) Access is also significantly affected by the "hidden curriculum," the process by which a student learns— or doesn't—how a school works, how to navigate in the system, how and when to ask for support, how to identify opportunities, how to present himself or herself for evaluation. It takes skill and confidence to create a successful application for admission, for support, for employment.

Fifth, student decisions about higher education are made in high school. Programs designed to influence those decisions must therefore address students while they are still in high school—but the sharp distinction between secondary and post-secondary education, coupled with the jurisdictional issue, makes it difficult to address access issues in an integrated and effective way.

THERE IS a story that Norman Riddell challenged Alex Usher to come up with research projects that would really show just how high school students might be influenced to enroll in post-secondary education. Usher went away and came back with a proposal for a series of groundbreaking pilot projects designed to test various approaches with different student populations. The projects would divide a random sample of students into experimental and control groups. The experimental groups would be given various kinds of enrichment—stimulation, counselling, financial aid and so forth—and their choices about post-secondary education would be compared with the choices of the control group who had received no enrichment at all. Which enhancements would encourage students to go on to higher education? Which ones would not?

"The main pilot projects were randomized field trials, with which everyone's familiar in medicine, but [which] are rarely done in education, and have almost never been done here," says Andrew Parkin. "They were very leading-edge—we lead the world in this kind of research, although we don't yet have many results. The main results will come out after the Foundation has closed.

"Together, the pilot projects were about a $45-million invest-ment over eight years. It was clearly the biggest single investment in research in one social policy area in Canada, outside medi-cine. I had two people running it—and these programs stretched from New Brunswick to Vancouver Island."

Randomized field trials are "the gold standard in research," says Jocelyn Charron, who manages several of the projects. But they are uncommon, because they normally face some serious obstacles. For one thing, this kind of social science research is often bedevilled by accusations of unfairness because some students receive inducements that are withheld from others. Furthermore, the Foundation's projects depended totally on the cooperation of the provinces, since they reached deep into provincial school systems, an area completely and inarguably within provincial jurisdiction.

By the time the projects began however, the Foundation's research activities had created such productive relationships with the provinces that neither of these issues caused any prob-lem at all. Indeed, teachers and provincial officials proved eager to participate, recognizing that they might benefit significantly from the process—as, in fact, they have.

Perhaps the most elaborate pilot project was Future to Dis-cover, which involved four thousand students in New Brunswick and one thousand in Manitoba. This was the program that had such an impact on the Babin family in Shediac. Another major initiative was the AVID program in British Columbia.

AVID stands for "Advancement Via Individual Determina-tion," and it had its origins in the wave of school integration that washed over the United States after the *Brown v. Board of Education* decision in 1954. The wave reached San Diego in 1979, when the courts ordered the school district to integrate its schools by bussing hundreds of disadvantaged students from impoverished inner-city neighbourhoods to middle-class suburban schools like Clairemont High.

Most teachers at Clairemont were apprehensive and resentful about the impending enrollment of five hundred underprivileged kids. The new students were mostly African-American and Hispanic, but they also included recent immigrants from Asia and Africa, many of whom spoke very little English. Some teachers transferred out of Clairemont. One teacher, however, saw the change as an opportunity. Her name was Mary Catherine Swanson.

Swanson started with one class of thirty-two students and a $7,000 grant. She organized the students in groups and enlisted college students as tutors. She and the tutors showed the students how to organize their work and their time, how to take notes, how to study effectively, how to manage their relationships with other teachers, how to overcome their own insecurities. Among her core principles was a commitment to inquiry rather than lecture—asking questions, and thus forcing students to research, clarify, analyze and synthesize material. In the AVID classroom, learning became a collaborative activity, conducted not in isolation, but in small groups and tutorials. She and her team also developed a program of "writing to learn," using the process of writing, discussing, editing and rewriting as a powerful learning technique.

According to their IQ tests, the Clairemont High AVID students were only of average intelligence, and a couple dropped out. At graduation, however, twenty-eight of the thirty remaining students were accepted at four-year universities—a success rate of 93 per cent, versus a national average of 31 per cent. By the time four years had passed, 170 students had passed through the AVID program, and all of them had gone to college.

The AVID story is told in detail by Jonathan Freedman in *Wall of Fame: One Teacher, One Class and the Power to Save Schools, and Transform Lives.* The program initially faced a shocking amount of opposition, but by 2004, AVID was serving more than 92,000 students in 1,650 middle and high schools. It was transforming entire schools. More than thirty thousand students had graduated from AVID programs, and 95 per cent had continued on to college. The program had spread to twenty-four states and sixteen countries.

Norman Riddell had done his graduate studies in the U.S., and so, says one of his colleagues, it was natural for him to reach across the border to network with U.S. organizations like the National Scholarship Providers Association. He went to California to visit the AVID Center and Mary Catherine Swanson. There he learned that one AVID site had been established in Canada—in British Columbia, in the Fraser Valley community of Chilliwack. The director of the Chilliwack program was Stan Watchorn.

"Norman Riddell and Jocelyn Charron came out and talked to us," Stan Watchorn says. "I remember very vividly an occasion at Vedder Middle School when Norman came into a tutorial class—and he was the head of the Foundation—and he sat down with a group of students in Grade 8 or Grade 9, and started asking them questions and working with them as a tutor. In the AVID tutorial, the function of the tutor is not to give answers, but to use the Socratic method of asking questions so that the students will search for and arrive at the answers themselves. Norman was fabulous at it, and the kids really enjoyed it.

"So then the Foundation put together the plan. They wanted to do this research, and because Chilliwack had implemented AVID, we were asked to provide some support to the other school districts as we got underway."

Right from the beginning, the project was a partnership between the Foundation, the AVID Center in San Diego, and the B.C. government. Research and empirically verified results have been crucial to AVID's success, so the AVID Center was happy to participate. The agreement provided that the costs of the project, including the project staff provided by the provincial government, would come from the Foundation. The province was eager to see the research extended to cover small rural high schools, which required a more complicated research design. For many months, the project's steering committee met by telephone at least weekly as the project unfolded.

Stan Watchorn eventually became the B.C. district director for AVID, overseeing a research project in twenty schools spread over fifteen school districts, ranging from suburban Vancouver to the Kootenays, the Cariboo and the Peace River. More than fifteen hundred students were involved—two-thirds of them in the AVID program and one-third serving as a control group. In the larger schools, the project enlisted two cohorts of students, with the first cohort graduating in 2009. The plan was to follow those students for another two years, which meant that the scientific results of the project would not be known until 2011 or 2012. By that time, the Foundation itself would have disappeared, but before it was dismantled it made provisions for the project's completion.

But Stan Watchorn didn't need the scientific reports to know that the project had an enormous impact. The official project included only two cohorts, who were in Grades 11 and 12 as he spoke. But every single school in the project, he noted, "has continued to recruit at the Grade 9 level and offer AVID beyond the research project. So the school itself has said, 'Yes, we think this is valuable and good for kids, and we'll continue it.'"

Stan remained the director of AVID B.C. after he became the principal of the high school in Hope, B.C., nestled among the soaring mountains right at the head of the Fraser Valley. There he proposed to reinvent his whole school using AVID's principles.

"Initially, when you first look into it, AVID seems to be targeted to creating post-secondary opportunities and successes for underserved students—kids in the middle," he said. "This is true, but fundamentally AVID is just good pedagogy. Just because these strategies are focusing on average kids who have academic potential doesn't mean that these strategies wouldn't work equally well—in terms of getting kids organized, learning how to take notes and so forth—with kids who *aren't* in the academic middle. It's just good pedagogy being supported and sustained over time.

"And there's another powerful aspect involved. AVID has the ability to change a school culture. AVID is about creating and supporting a comprehensive professional development program for staff which addresses teaching practices, a rigorous curriculum and the social and emotional support that students need to be successful. It's about creating a learning community within a school."

The Foundation's pilot-project managers, like Jocelyn Charron, were in Montreal, and they had to manage the projects from afar. They relied very heavily on people like Stan Watchorn who were immersed in the projects on the site.

144

"It's pretty amazing to discover how much talent there is in our education system," Jocelyn says. "That has been, for me, a great discovery. Of course projects like this attract people who want to make a difference. Still, I've met some very dedicated educators—and it's been quite inspiring for us. I think it speaks well of our education system that there's people like that in it."

THE FOUNDATION'S research program included several other pilot projects, notably a program of support and mentoring in three Ontario community colleges called Foundations for Success, and a program in Manitoba oriented towards aboriginal students called Making Education Work. But perhaps the most ambitious and complex project was LE,NO<u>N</u>ET (pronounced "lee-*non*-git," a Straits Salish word which means "success after enduring many hardships"), a program at the University of Victoria aimed at enhancing the university experience for First Nations students and addressing the issues that often cause aboriginal students to drop out.

That very conception of the situation, however, is probably part of the problem. The phrasing subtly suggests that the university is fixed and monolithic, like a formation of intellectual bedrock, and that success, for a student, means adjusting oneself to that stony reality. Aboriginal students have difficulty adjusting and must therefore be assisted.

The reality is infinitely more complicated than that and it reflects a relationship between aboriginal culture and conventional Western education that contains elements of tragedy as well as the prospect of redemption. For the European tradition, knowledge is largely about action, about controlling and shaping society and the environment through the techniques of engineering, science, architecture, medicine, jurisprudence and other disciplines.

But that is not the aboriginal view of knowledge.

"The goal of indigenous education," writes Gregory Cajete in *Look to the Mountain: An Ecology of Indigenous Education*, "is to be fully knowledgeable about one's place in the universe or spirituality. This is often realized through the structures of daily practices as well as in sacred art, ceremonies, rituals and dances, all in reflection of nature's cycles." The quotation appears in LE,NO̱NET's handbook for SFACT (Staff and Faculty Aboriginal Cultural Training), a program that reflects the understanding that if aboriginal students are to succeed at universities, the students will have to change—but so will the universities.

SFACT, which is directed at the university's employees, is one of seven components of LE,NO̱NET. The other six components are directed at aboriginal students. They include special bursaries for students in financial need as well as emergency funding of up to $750 per student per year. The emergency funding is designed to accommodate special aboriginal needs. When a relative dies, for instance, family members are expected to attend the memorial ceremonies. To fail in this obligation can be a very serious matter. So the aboriginal student leaves the university and goes home—and then doesn't have the money to come back and finish the year. The emergency funding solves that problem.

"Another example," says Yvonne Rondeau, the manager of the project, "is where students are told, Oh, you're going to get X amount of funding from your band or some other source, so they sign up, they register and they get here—and then their funding gets cut, halfway through a term. Then what do they do? So the emergency relief fund is able to respond to those needs."

A third service to students is a mentoring program.

"When I think back on my first year here, it was overwhelming," says Amanda Laliberté, a tall, graceful young woman with a pronounced baby bump. "It's very intimidating. It's a big campus, and there are lots of people. So I had a mentor, and she was there to guide me along if I had any questions about the campus. And then later I was a mentor myself."

"Mentors are there to communicate with their students via email or by phone, or you can have coffee," Yvonne explains.

"Sometimes they meet with their students just once at the start of the year for an orientation and that's it, but other times there's continual contact, and in some instances it's become quite intense with the mentor when the student has had real crises."

LE,NONET also sponsors a monthly "writing circle," as well as drop-in luncheons, craft nights and movie nights. An important objective of the program is the creation of a sense of community for aboriginal students on campus.

The most innovative features of LE,NONET are its community internships and research apprenticeships, both of which carry a $3,500 stipend as well as 1.5 units of course credit. A preparation seminar, open only to aboriginal students involved with LE,NONET, provides basic instruction in research ethics as well as cultural preparation for working in settings ranging from rural reserves to urban aboriginal organizations. Students must obtain a B grade, with 80 per cent attendance. Amanda Laliberté attended the very first seminar.

"It was the very first class that I'd taken in indigenous studies," she remembers. "It was definitely an eye-opener, some of the material that we learned with regard to residential schools, the effects of colonization, shame around identity—lots of things that I hadn't thought about. It was a really safe space, with other students that had experienced similar things."

Not all faculties were eager to accept these credits, however, nor was the university easily persuaded to recognize an internship or apprenticeship stretching over two terms for only 1.5 credits, although that seems a very minor adjustment by way of recognizing a different cultural reality. Yvonne Rondeau laughs as she recalls a visitor who reported that Yukon College had adjusted its actual school year to accommodate the reality that many of its aboriginal students were partially reliant on hunting for survival and simply would not be able to attend classes during hunting season.

The internships involve two hundred hours of work in a community setting, either in an aboriginal community or with an urban aboriginal organization. Some students have done internships on campus or worked with nearby organizations like the Saanich Indian School Board. Others travel far afield. One student spent the summer working on native governance in the Six Nations in Ontario.

Amanda Laliberté did a community internship with an organization that partners with aboriginal groups to provide adventure therapy by means of kayaking and similar activities.

"It was great, because I was able to do my summer studies and go on a couple of trips with them. I went on a sea-kayaking trip with the Saanich Indian Tribal School through the Gulf Islands and had an opportunity to learn a bit more about the people that are from the territory here—because I am a visitor here, and it was important for me to learn a bit more about the local territory and people."

A visitor?

"Actually, I'm from . . ."—she laughs—"Um, where am I from? Originally from Saskatchewan, but I've been out here for about five years, mostly in Nanaimo. I'm Metis, on my father's side of the family."

Amanda also did a research apprenticeship, which required two hundred hours of hands-on research on a subject of the student's choosing, under the guidance of a faculty adviser—and the faculty adviser had to have completed the SFACT training. The impact of SFACT on the advisers is sometimes profound. One adviser, Dr. Kelly Bannister, said that her experience with LE,NONET "was one of the most meaningful experiences I had at UVic. I have heard others say the same. The importance and significance of LE,NONET is tremendous, for all kinds of individuals as well as the university as a whole."

Shades of Stan Watchorn. LE,NONET turns out to be about creating a learning community within the university—with the further wrinkle that the university has committed to continuing the LE,NONET programs that have proven to be successful.

With the research apprenticeships, the topic is often related to the student's field of concentration, but not always. One physics student, for instance, had heard stories about an aboriginal opera that had been written and performed in Duncan, B.C., in the middle of the twentieth century, and dedicated his research apprenticeship to finding out the truth of the matter and the fate of the opera. Others have undertaken projects in medicine, linguistics, botany, addiction, indigenous governments and so forth.

Amanda did her research apprenticeship working with a professor of anthropology on the preliminary research for a contemporary Salish exhibition for the Art Gallery of Greater Victoria, and also on the long-ago history of a relatively progressive day-school for native children in Oliver, B.C. The experience opened her eyes, she says, to the fascination of research.

"It was like a treasure hunt!" she cries. "Sometimes it was really frustrating—but then again you'll find something that's just really exciting! I built a long-lasting relationship with that professor, and I've actually been talking with her about doing a master's." She smiles, patting her tummy. "Well, the baby will be born, and I'll take a year off, but then I'd like to come back and pursue an interdisciplinary master's degree in visual arts and anthropology."

LE,NONET is obviously a groundbreaking program, but how did its components add up to a Foundation research project? The University of Victoria has about nine hundred aboriginal students, about 139 of whom have participated in LE,NONET.

The analysis would compare the drop-out and graduation rates for students who were supported by LE,NONET to the rates for aboriginal students who did not have that support.

That's quantitative analysis, but the project had an equally interesting qualitative dimension. For traditional educational researchers, the measure of success is whether or not a student persists and graduates—but is that the right definition of success for aboriginals? And, as Norman Riddell points out, that very question challenged some of the fundamental assumptions of the research.

"We went in saying, 'We're going to increase aboriginal persistence and we're going to graduate them with the credentials,'" he recalls "And what we discovered is that aboriginal Canadians don't necessarily have the same view of success. To some extent they do, but they're much less 'credentialist' than we are, and they said, 'If I got something valuable at university in the first year-and-a-half that I could use in my community and dropped out and went and used it in my community, that's success.' And that's something we're going to have to struggle within that project in writing the final reports. We've come to have a more sophisticated idea of what success is. So our vision of success changes; the students change, but we change too."

REFLECTING ON the innovative research projects that he supervised—AVID, Future to Discover, LE,NONET and all—Andrew Parkin remarks on the Foundation's commitment to the dispassionate pursuit of knowledge.

Intellectually, he says, the pilot projects raised "the standard of research on education in Canada by a considerable degree. That's still not quite as visible as it will be once all the reports are up. But the desire to invest in research that is really substantive, and to do it knowing that we may not get the answers that we want—that's what's most striking, because a lot of people do research in order to get the answers they want. You do a poll and you write the questions in such a way to show that everyone agrees with you—and that's research.

"But to really move away from that and take the risk that you will invest significantly in research and get answers that make you uncomfortable—that, I think, is a credit to the people who thought the idea up and a credit to the board of directors who approved it. I didn't start these projects up. I wasn't working in educational economics before, and I don't have experience with that type of applied research. So my own experience is one of just being impressed."

Parkin was also impressed by the incidental, unexpected benefits of the projects.

"The idea wasn't to energize a group of teachers so that they would then, through the rest of their professional careers, be able to draw from experiences beyond what they would normally have had as teachers. That's the unintended consequence—but sometimes the unintended consequence is the one that sticks. These educators who have been involved with these projects have done incredible work with these students, and they will go on and do incredible work elsewhere. That's a really invisible side of what the Foundation has done."

The objective of the pilot projects was to increase our store of knowledge. But—as the impact on the teachers, the students, and the Babin family demonstrates—simply asking the right questions can produce profound changes. It is also striking that every project seemed to identify the same elements in effective pedagogy—active research and problem solving, writing and editing, creating presentations, working collaboratively, apprenticing and mentoring, internships and practical experience. Students exposed to that kind of active learning invariably do better than those who have simply been the passive recipients of lectures.

THE CAPACITY to do dispassionate research, says the August Personage, is actually another benefit of the Foundation structure.

"I think that research is an inherently governmental activity," he explains, crunching his bruschetta. "But it's a governmental activity that was not being done by government, unfortunately. There isn't very much research or available information about how these student aid organizations pursue their responsibilities, or what the needs are. When you try to get a sense of the demand—what is the demand for student loans and such?—there isn't very much data out there. So this is a major contribution to knowledge, in having had an institution like the Foundation collect the data from the provinces and massage it and use it. The data is all provincial, and you need someone to be able to pull it together, and take a national perspective in bringing it together."

Yves Pelletier, who managed the Future to Discover project, believes that a major feature of the Foundation's legacy is that "we've redefined how we look at access. Access has always been identified in Canada as being financial. But all the research on barriers has allowed us to shape things more profoundly than if we had just been a grant-giving organization."

Former board chair Gérard Veilleux also sees the research program as a huge part of the Foundation's legacy.

"What I find amazing is that the best research in the field of student assistance was done by a federally funded organization,"

Veilleux reflects. "That is an unbelievable achievement." Yes, he concedes, education is a provincial responsibility. Fine. "But somehow ten large governments, ten large departments of education, ten large programs of student assistance—and yet very little research had been done, and it took a federal initiative to do that research, without creating any constitutional or jurisdictional issue. I think that is an immense accomplishment, and I hope it will be seen as a model that can be replicated in other areas."

The importance of educational access to a twenty-first-century nation can hardly be overstated, says Yves Pelletier. In the new, evolving economy, "everyone has to be able to go on to post-secondary education. There has to be social equity, and there are long-term economic gains for the country if you actually get everyone with a certain form of post-secondary education."

The new Canada needs a smart and skillful population. Providing access to post-secondary education—for everyone—is the only policy that will provide us with one.

› Polyvalente La Samare, Plessisville, Quebec

. . . .

I T'S LIKE Hollywood.

The presenter steps up to the microphone and gives the names of the nominees. Their faces appear on the big flat screen that faces the audience. The presenter announces the winner, and the crowd erupts in cheers and whistles. A spotlight pans across the audience, locks onto the winner and follows that person down the aisle to the stage, where an usher steers the winner up to the stage. The happy recipient accepts the envelope while the audience hoots and claps.

But it's not Hollywood. It's the auditorium at a high school called Polyvalente La Samare in Plessisville, Quebec. "La Samare" is the Biblical woman of Samaria, and "polyvalente" is a lovely word, derived from chemistry, denoting multiple connections. There doesn't seem to be any direct English translation, but this is a comprehensive regional school, serving several communities. And the event is an awards night. The presenters are handing out scholarships.

The trim, youthful man on the stage right now is Stéphane LeBlanc, senior awards officer with the Foundation. He is here to present Millennium Excellence Awards to three graduating students: Sophie Boutin, Cloé Marcoux and Mathieu Samson. Stéphane reminds the assembly that these awards recognize not only academic achievement, but also good citizenship and proven leadership. Because the Foundation is winding down, this is the last round of Excellence Awards to be distributed, ever.

Stéphane now reveals to the crowd an astonishing fact: that over the past decade, this smallish rural school has produced more than fifty Excellence Award laureates—more than any other public high school in Canada. The auditorium erupts in cheers and whistles.

In fact, the only school of any kind to win more awards than this modest public high school in the Eastern Townships of Quebec is Lester B. Pearson College of the Pacific, the only Canadian school in the rarefied international network of twelve United World Colleges. La Samare has not only topped all the public schools in Canada, but it has also captured more scholarships—often *far* more scholarships—than such prestigious private institutions as the University of Toronto Schools, Upper Canada College, Bishop Strachan School, Ridley College, St. John's-Ravenscourt School. It has produced as many as eight laureates in a single year.

How has La Samare accomplished this remarkable feat?

Through its intense relationship with the whole community, says Danielle Béliveau, La Samare's directrice, or principal. Plessisville is a small town of about nine thousand people, "so there's not very much to do, and the school becomes the centre of the community. It's where people do a lot of their activities." What kinds of activities? Non-credit courses, meetings of clubs and associations, festivals, shows, fundraisers—all manner of projects and gatherings. The school, she smiles, is in use from early morning till late at night, seven days a week, and that very fact draws people in. The janitor, for example, seeing the students and teachers working on projects together late into the evening, decided that he too would like to volunteer. He now coaches the basketball team.

With an enrollment of just over one thousand, La Samare is the perfect size, says guidance counsellor Patricia Bourque— large enough to offer any activity that's in demand, but small enough that people know one another very personally. It's the only school in the region where teachers and guidance counsellors work as a team. Because roughly 80 per cent of the teachers were also students here—as were the local doctors, lawyers and business people, as was Patricia herself—they fully understand and support the tradition of community involvement. And they know its effect on the students.

When you think back on your school years, asks Béliveau, what do you remember? Maybe a couple of teachers and a course or two, but mainly you remember plays, clubs, sports, friends, committees that you served on, trips that you took. La Samare's philosophy is that it's everything *outside* the classroom that makes students love school, so the school lays great emphasis on providing a complete spectrum of extracurricular activities to complement its academic offerings. As a result, says Béliveau, while comparable schools have a dropout rate of about 25 per cent, La Samare's dropout rate is around 5 per cent to 6 per cent.

"When I first came to an awards ceremony at La Samare," says Stéphane LeBlanc, "I noticed that parents, grandparents, siblings and community mentors all participated. It was clear that the school, community and volunteer sector had a very symbiotic relationship, and that this wasn't new. And all the students mentioned the immense support they received from their parents, teachers and guidance counsellors.

"Actually, I had already seen that support. Back at the beginning of the program, I used to get phone calls from a teacher named Majella Lemieux at La Samare. He'd have questions about the criteria, and about the application form. What exactly did we mean by such-and-such? What sort of information should an application provide about something else? He'd thank me very politely each time, and then these great applications started to come in from Plessisville."

Majella Lemieux is a slight, intense, good-humoured man, now retired. For him, the essence of a teacher's calling is to know the students profoundly, not just as faces in rows of desks, but as unique individuals with passions and problems—and to support them fiercely.

"Kids can do marvellous things, but you have to push them," he says. "And if you push them, you have to support them, you have to be there. The best way to know them is to participate with them in activities. It doesn't take that much time. Many student organizations meet after school, and I liked to be ready for the next day, so I didn't leave until five o'clock or five-thirty. They were just down the corridor, so I'd look in on them, see how they were doing, help them if they needed it.

"And if you're there, and they have personal problems or whatever, that's when they come to talk to you. And that's when you get them! After that you don't have problems in the classroom. But if you're not there, you never get them."

That kind of knowledge about the students, says Patricia Bourque, is essential. Even if they know about scholarships, which they often don't, students will hesitate to apply because they think they aren't special. The teacher or counsellor must provide information—but must also help students to see themselves more objectively, to recognize their own achievements. Simply filling out an application makes students reflect on what they've actually done and teaches them important lessons about presenting themselves not just to scholarship committees, but to admissions committees and employers as well.

Plessisville is the chief town in the Comté de l'Érable–Maple County, so named for its sugar maple industry, which exports to thirty-five countries. La Samare is not the only facility that Plessisville provides for its youth; another is a *maison des jeunes,* one of 135 such youth centres scattered around the province. There are no *maisons des jeunes* in the smaller communities that surround Plessisville and that provide about half the students of La Samare–Notre-Dame-de-Lourdes, Villeroy, Laurierville, Sainte-Sophie-d'Halifax, Inverness, Saint-Pierre-Baptiste and Lyster. But those small communities have given rise to an even more remarkable incubator for youth.

Partenaires 12–18 began in Lyster about fifteen years ago, says Gilles Cayer, the organization's coordinator, a compact, dynamic man in his forties. A group of parents, disturbed by such obvious signs of youthful discontent as vandalism, drinking and drug use, approached the municipality looking for help. The municipality agreed to provide a space and staff time to help youths and adults get together.

The group then did a brilliant and simple thing. They asked the young people what they needed—and they listened deeply to the answers.

The kids said they wanted sports and recreation, trips and similar activities. Very well, said the adults. How can we get those things? Let's organize. You lead, and we'll support you. The result was a partnership of youth, parents, the municipality, local businesses and others designed to "foster independence, initiative and a sense of responsibility among young people of 12 to 18 years."

Coached by the adults, the young people learned to create organizations, set goals, make and execute action plans. Responsibility is addictive; as you learn to exercise it, you want more of it. As the teenagers gained confidence and experience, they took on more daunting challenges—creating peer-mentorship networks and counselling services such as suicide watches. They identified a need for jobs, particularly in the summer, and realized that the local business community couldn't possibly employ them all, so they studied entrepreneurship and began creating their own micro-businesses.

As similar committees sprang up in nearby communities, the organization set up an office in La Samare. It drew grants and sponsorships from companies, development agencies, the Ministry of Health, foundations, the school board and the police. One foundation official, visiting from Montreal, was stunned to see fourteen-year-olds confidently engaged in organizational development, knowing how to run meetings, take minutes, create boards of directors and so on. He was "on a cloud," grins Gilles Cayer. "He said he had never seen anything like it."

Cayer views himself not as an animator, but as an "accompagnateur"—someone who accompanies the young people on their journeys. What's visible to the community, he says, are the social, cultural and sporting activities, but what's at least as important is the constant counselling both between the young people and with others. One example is Cayer's own practice of encouraging students to apply for Millennium Excellence Awards.

Partenaires 12–18 is committed to three community objectives: meeting the specific needs of rural youth, alleviating the social problems caused by the decay of rural communities and retaining young people in their communities. The model ultimately spread far beyond the Comté de L' Érable, spawning sister organizations across Quebec.

And what about its effects in its birthplace? Delinquency has dropped almost to zero, says Cayer. And not long ago, Partenaires 12–18 was the subject of a scientific study. He stresses the word "scientific." The study showed that of the young people who had been involved in Partenaires 12–18, a very large proportion returned to their communities after studying elsewhere. More than 66 per cent remained seriously involved in community service, no matter where they eventually settled. The proportion who regularly voted in elections was over 90 per cent, as opposed to about 50 per cent in their age group. More than 90 per cent were proud to have been recognized for their achievements, and that recognition had motivated them to continue.

And two of the students presented with Excellence Awards by Stéphane LeBlanc were participants in Partenaires 12–18: Sophie Boutin and Cloé Marcoux.

There's a moral to the story of La Samare and Partenaires 12–18 and their community, and it is this: rural communities that want to survive should put the development of their young people at the very top of their agendas. The heart of that development is respect and responsibility. A few short years after graduation, the teenager will emerge as a scientist, a teacher, an entrepreneur, a doctor—an adult citizen with a major contribution to make. If such young people grow up believing that the community truly belongs to them, that they are respected and trusted as well as cared for, that the community provides the soil in which they personally can flower—if those things are true, then the chances are good that those young adults will decide that they want to raise their own children in that same secure and fertile environment.

It's a virtuous circle, and it begins with the school and the community, and the partnership between them. In the end, La Samare's astonishing record of winning scholarships is not so much an achievement in itself as a dramatic indicator of community well-being.

"If the school activities would stop tomorrow, the community would slowly die off, because it's such an integral part of what the community is," says Danielle Béliveau. The relationship between the school and the community, she says, is not one of give-and-take, but one of give-and-give.

Conversations in Plessisville are peppered with the word "give." You give to the community; the community gives back to you. You give responsibility to young people. People give their time. You give guidance. Students give you their confidence.

Everyone has a set of gifts, says community-development philosopher John McKnight. The good community is one in which those gifts can be given.

Bien sûr. That's how it works in Plessisville.

> *six*

THE GHOST FOUNDATION

. . . .

T HERE HAD never been any guarantee that the
Foundation would continue beyond its legis-
lated ten years, and nobody had forgotten the
tempests that surrounded its creation. But, as the end of the
Foundation's ten-year mandate approached, the provinces—once
the Foundation's most bitter critics—began to feel nervous about
its future. The Foundation had been created by a Liberal administration. Would a Conservative government renew its mandate? If
not, what—if anything—would replace it?

"We have a group called the Intergovernmental Consultative
Committee on Student Financial Assistance," says Tom Glenwright, executive director of Manitoba Student Aid. "The ICCSFA
basically is all the student aid directors across Canada, plus our
colleagues in the Canada Student Loans Program. When I was
chair of ICCSFA a couple of years ago, we got together and produced a paper asking the feds to keep the Foundation going. We
knew it was a losing battle, but all of us were involved in crafting
this paper and putting it forward to the feds and arguing that the

Foundation should be allowed to continue. It was all the provincial and territorial jurisdictions together, and we really believed that we'd all be better off if we got another ten-year commitment from the federal government for the Foundation."

The ICCSFA paper specifically noted the Foundation's individualized relationships with the provinces and territories as opposed to the one-size-fits-all approach of the Canada Student Loans Program. The demise of the Foundation, it said, would end "a funding mechanism that allows for jurisdictions to respond to diverse needs and circumstances." The distribution of Millennium bursaries through individual agreements with all the provinces and territories "allows funding to be allocated in different ways to meet diverse challenges and goals" and "has afforded jurisdictions the flexibility to deliver funds in a manner that more effectively addresses challenges in particular jurisdictions and responds to regional diversity."

Translation: We really like the Foundation's policy of reaching the common goal of helping needy students by using varied methods that fit the unique situations of individual provinces. And we think that approach yields better results than a general formula mechanically applied across the country.

Picking up on these sentiments, Canwest News Service reported just before the budget announcement that "there is a feeling among provincial governments [that] the program is working well and there appears to be little appetite to dismantle it or to divert the money to another federal student aid venture."

New Brunswick Minister of Education Kelly Lamrock was then chair of the Council of Ministers of Education of Canada. "Given that the federal government has not indicated to us that they are doing any serious thinking about reform," he said. "I would be surprised and disappointed if there were huge changes to the status quo. I think it would be an unfortunate move to take that step."

Ten days later, on February 26, 2008, the Government of Canada took that step.

In his budget address, Finance Minister Jim Flaherty announced that the government would wind down the Canada Millennium Scholarship Foundation by early 2010. Said Flaherty: "Our Government is investing in a new consolidated post-secondary Canada Student Grants Program. It will be a single-focused program that fully respects provincial jurisdiction. It will also provide more effective support to more students for more years of study.

"As the Canada Millennium Scholarship Foundation winds down, our Government will provide $350 million for this Canada Student Grants Program in 2009–10, growing to $430 million in 2012–13. In comparison to the predecessor programs, this funding will reach an estimated 245,000 students. This is over 100,000 more students from low- and middle-income families than the current system."

The Foundation was finished. The Foundation's staff was stunned.

They had found creative ways to work with the provinces, and they had built a national network of young leaders. The Foundation had developed a successful, responsive suite of programs, and it had held its administrative costs down to 4 per cent of expenditures—and used those administrative savings to pay for additional scholarships and also for the pioneering research effort. The staff felt, understandably, that the Foundation had been efficient, innovative and responsible. And now this.

Some have argued that the Foundation had been somewhat complacent and even a touch naive, knowing it was doing a good job and assuming that others would therefore support it. Indeed, not everyone involved with the Foundation was convinced that renewal was even a good idea; perhaps the Foundation had worked well precisely because it knew its lifespan was short. Riddell had been resolutely opposed to any use of the students to promote the organization, although Jean Chrétien himself later expressed surprise that the hundreds of thousands of students who had been served by the Foundation had not risen up in its defence. Overall, the Foundation had not shown the visceral instinct for self-preservation that characterizes most organizations.

"I'm not sure that we would hold the view that it would have been appropriate to develop such an instinct," says Norman Riddell. "The point of view of the board was that they were given money, and a task, by the Parliament of Canada, and their job was to do that task as best they could. They were not there to tell Parliament what it should do. So this had a very real effect on how the Foundation approached its renewal.

"We never went around saying, 'You've got to renew the Foundation.' We went around saying, 'Non-repayable student financial assistance is absolutely essential. An excellence award program that recognizes young people and contributes to their personal development so that they can become leaders of tomorrow—that's really important. It's really important to understand how financial assistance actually plays out, and it's really important to be testing new initiatives carefully through pilot projects. Research is really important.'

"But we weren't saying, 'It has to be us.' Because we were given a job, and that's what the board concentrated on, all the time. So if that's your perspective, you don't seek your self-preservation—it's your mission you care about. And the board made that distinction constantly."

Not everyone agrees with the board's decision that it should go gentle into the political night. Norman Riddell draws a sharp distinction between the mission and the organization. The success of the mission matters; the survival of the organization does not. But perhaps the issue is not so simple.

If one believes not only in the mission but also in the effectiveness of the organization in addressing the mission, then perhaps the organization needed to ensure that its activities and its character were fully known and understood. Do Canadians—for example—really not want a national program of Excellence Awards? Did they even really know that the program existed, as they certainly know about the Rhodes Scholarships? Isn't there a legitimate argument that the program—*in the service of the mission*—should have been promoted and branded and celebrated? And wouldn't that promotion in itself have inspired some young Canadians to make themselves eligible for it? Do Canadians, even to this day, know what they lost?

"I think the Foundation had a marketing problem, and especially a branding problem," says one political operative. "They were doing two very different things—one of which was the excellence program and the other was the general bursaries, right? Now someone else can take care of the general bursaries—the provinces, this new organization, whoever—but you need a national body to build this network of leaders. If you just had a national body working on the network of leaders, that would have been your Rhodes Scholarship, and everybody in the country would have recognized it.

"So Millennium didn't become important enough for Canadians. And that's the Foundation's fault, for not marketing it properly."

Very diplomatically, former Saskatchewan premier Allan Blakeney agrees. A long-serving member of the board, Blakeney has finely tuned political instincts, and he doesn't buy the argument that bursary winners couldn't have been used to promote the program.

"I had a little row in the board about that," Blakeney says. "I know the idea is that these people got these scholarships by proving that they are poor—I'm overstating this—and therefore we should not be advertising who they are. But, forgive me, I don't think they care. I think that they would not resent us distributing their names. I think we should have put on the application, 'Do you object to us providing your name to your Member of Parliament?' I wanted to supply the Members of Parliament with all of these names, so that their offices could send letters of congratulation—not for winning the scholarship, but for going ahead with post-secondary education, which we think is a good thing for young people, and a good thing for our country. And this is a program of the Government of Canada of which we are all proud, and so on.

"So I wanted to see if we could get the MPs to pump these out and then try to see if we could half-induce the students or the parents to write a little note to the MP saying, 'We're very happy that the Government of Canada saw fit to help.' I hadn't figured out how to do that part, quite—but you know, I was in this business myself, and I know how MPs think. If you get these semi-unsolicited letters, letters that the senders have to sit down and write, then you know that these people are conscious that this money is coming from the taxes they pay, and they think it's a good use of taxes, because their kid's getting the money.

"This was kind of a hobby horse of mine for two or three years. But I couldn't convince the board."

By early 2008, in any case, the government had spoken. The mission—or parts of it—would continue. But the Foundation's story was over.

After the budget announcement, Norman Riddell convened a meeting of the staff. He "gave a speech to all of us," remembers one young staffer, "and then at a certain point his voice cracked, and he was really visibly moved, and it was just very touching. Like, you could just sort of tell that he really cared about the people that worked here, and he really wanted to let us know that, no matter what, we would be well taken care of."

Riddell's response to the government's decision was characteristically rational and clear, however complex his emotions may have been. What do we do? Wind up our work in an orderly way and try to find other organizations to complete what must be left unfinished. Find ways to preserve the lessons we have learned— about student aid, about federalism, about access, about social policy research, about leadership. Ensure that everything possible is done to ease the transition for the staff, who will lose their jobs. Leave the office neat and tidy when we lock the doors.

The good news, clearly, was that the federal government had accepted that it should maintain a very substantial presence in the field of financial aid for needy students, an idea that was not at all entrenched when the Foundation came into being. Canadian students would continue to be supported, and indeed, many more of them would be helped. In fact, the additional support from the government would be invested in non-repayable loans for low-income students, which the Foundation had been advocating for years. The overarching fact was that the federal government had made a huge commitment to supporting Canadian students, especially the most needy ones, and it may be argued that having established and demonstrated the value of such support, the Foundation had actually served its most important purpose.

"Even in those first few years, we never thought necessarily it was going to be forever," says Franca Gucciardi. "We thought it was going to be ten years. We just thought, we have ten years—and a lot of money. We can do a lot that will change the fabric and the knowledge base in the country for these issues. And I think the Foundation did that. We really need to focus on the fact that it did accomplish what it was meant to accomplish, regardless of the fact that it won't be continued. Renewal was never the intention when we started out, and the Foundation shouldn't be judged by that."

What is lost on the bursary front is the flexibility that allowed the Foundation to tailor its Access Bursaries to the needs of individual provinces, and the extremely efficient administrative processes that the Foundation had developed. The sophisticated computer systems that allowed Randolf Harrold to sift out potential wpc bursary recipients by field of study and institution—the only systems that could track bursary recipients across the country—those systems constitute an expensive asset that will be, in effect, simply discarded. They will go to the National Archives, where they may be useful for historical research but not for current management.

"My view," says the August Personage, "is that once you've got this Foundation set up, even if it's not exactly what you want, why would you want to destroy it, and then recreate it somewhere else? That makes no sense to me whatsoever. I'm pretty small-c conservative on this, and I would say, 'Go with what you've got.' The transaction costs of setting up a new organization in government are *massive*—and having to recreate all the systems and the controls and everything? It's *nuts!*"

AS THE Foundation's ten-year mandate drew to a close, the future of the Foundation's research program was unclear.

At first it seemed destined to disappear, but in April 2009, the University of Victoria unveiled a proposal to create a

Canadian research network on post-secondary education access and success, an independent network of researchers across the country linked to an administrative hub in Victoria. It would cost $10.5 million annually, and its research program would focus on five areas: identification of the research questions that needed to be addressed, analysis of barriers and incentives for access and success, program evaluation, pilot projects and dissemination of information.

If that list sounds familiar, it's because these issues had been the Foundation's research concerns as well. Indeed, the new network would "begin with as seamless a transition as possible from the existing Millennium Research Program to the new research network in order to ensure continuity, efficiency, and continued momentum."

The continuity, said Norman Riddell, was important.

"If the research isn't continued, there's a loss of momentum," says Norman Riddell. "We've gotten to a point where we can do certain things that we couldn't have done initially. If it collapses, and we go through a certain period when it isn't done, all the work that we had to do to build it up will have to be done again."

THE EXCELLENCE Awards Program, which was building a national cadre of educated and experienced leadership, has simply vanished—and will have to be recreated if it's ever to be done again.

"Again, if you don't run it for three or four years, you're back at ground zero," says Riddell. "There's nobody who's able to come up with $15 million a year, which is what you need to run this program, except the Government of Canada. It's not expensive, and I think it's a great, great benefit—but they don't see it as *theirs*."

Fifteen million dollars truly is not a great deal of money to foster a whole generation of leaders. You could pay that much for a single house in Vancouver. Leading corporations pay that much in annual compensation to their CEOs. If Canada can't find that much to nurture its very best young people, then the country is impoverished in more ways than one.

Meanwhile, the chief visible legacy of the Excellence Awards Program will be the Millennium Alumni Network, an electronic linkage connecting more than two thousand alumni "through the exchange of knowledge, the creation of new opportunities and through a shared passion and commitment to excellence," as the network's website puts it. During its final years, the Foundation made a strenuous effort to involve its alumni in its programming, calling on them to assess applications and volunteer at conferences while also encouraging the development of the network itself.

The network officially came into being in 2006 and included alumni in Quebec, Cambodia, Winnipeg, Edmonton, England, Ottawa, Vancouver and Boston. Its members were graduate students, parliamentary interns, communications officers, future doctors, world travellers and outdoor enthusiasts, and their announced passions included family law, the aluminum industry and HIV/AIDS.

"They're basically trying to build a learning organization," says Chad Lubelsky, who has been coaching the group. "What you've called 'the glue' that holds the group together, they've been calling 'the generative force.' What they have in common is not only that they've all held Excellence Awards, but also that they have strong shared values around making communities better places, and they have a lot of learning about that, but the learning isn't necessarily connected.

"So they're trying to connect their collective learnings and make them available as a body of knowledge that people can draw on and contribute to, and that all of them can use in their own community work. So if your organization needs help writing a business plan, the network will have people who can help with that—and they could even be hired to help do it."

"What's amazing about this network," says Dan Jacobs, an alumnus who now works in the leadership development programs of Telus, "is that this is a place where you get reinvigorated. Every couple of months you're connected with other leaders who are highly involved, highly motivated—and that's why I'm here, this is what I'm interested in. The common interest here is leadership and community engagement. What makes Millennium unique is that it engages people at a young age who are then going to be connected twenty years from now."

We're sitting at a table in a Montreal hotel conference room with about ninety alumni, all focused on building their new network.

"Imagine this group here in this room, twenty years from now," says Dan, waving his hand. "We'll all be in different industries—business or medicine or agriculture or education. People always stress the importance of building relationships, but what if those relationships have existed for fifteen or twenty years? And it's just a matter of picking up the phone to get in touch with any of these incredible people?"

And, Chad notes, these young alumni are in a process of personal transformation. In university, they had a lot of social support, but in the workplace the same support may be hard to find. The network can help to fill that gap. In a sense, the network is "the re-creation of a tribe," with all the benefits and comforts that implies. And the impact of that tribe on the wider Canadian community could be as powerful as the energies of the young people who are creating it.

AFTER THE Foundation's dissolution, the broad access agenda will be carried by a new organization, the Canadian Post-Secondary Access Partnership, created in 2007 by the Foundation and the YMCA of Greater Toronto, acting on behalf of local YMCAS across the country.

"As we increasingly recognized that you needed more than money to get people into post-secondary education, we began to recognize that it was going to be more than government as well," says Riddell. "And that meant looking at how civil society could play a role in motivating and supporting access particularly of the under-represented populations. This partnership really is Canadian civil society at work, largely under the leadership of the YMCA."

The partnership's targets are students who are the first in their families to attend post-secondary education, as well as low-income, aboriginal and other students who are currently under-represented in higher education. The idea is to use the Y's presence across the country to provide workshops, advice and mentoring both at the Y and in the schools, and to both adult learners and teens. The objective is to make potential students more aware of post-secondary education, help them find suitable post-secondary opportunities and give them the skills they need to succeed when they get there. The programs are also aimed at parents, providing them with the knowledge they need to be good coaches and supporters for their children.

The YMCA, says Diana Wickham, the Foundation's executive officer for development, "has terrific partners at the local level, outreach into all kinds of communities, a whole array of existing programs directed at youth and adults. They have employment programs and newcomer programs and youth leadership programs as well as their recreational programs. They were the founders of Sir George Williams University, so they have a long history of involvement in education." It's true: that university— now a part of Concordia University—was actually named for the founder of the YMCA.

The Foundation's contribution to the partnership will be to create tools and workshops based on the what the Foundation learned from the Millennium pilot projects and also to train YMCA staff and others in their use. The partnership will also adapt training materials and resources from the U.S. National College Access Network.

By mid-2008, the partnership had already enlisted Ernst & Young as its first corporate sponsor and Ryerson University as its first institutional member. Its programs were being piloted at sixteen YMCA locations in a dozen cities stretching from Prince George and Vancouver to Halifax and St. John's, with multiple sites in Toronto and Montreal. In each location, the organization was seeking to enlist local school districts, colleges and universities, community organizations, aboriginal groups, ethnic communities, government and the private sector.

"Since then," says Diana Wickham, "the partnership with Ernst & Young has really started to have legs. They're putting money into the partnership, but in addition they're mobilizing their employees in their offices everywhere that the Y has a pilot site. So the YMCA has been training Ernst & Young employees as volunteers in this project." The hope is that other corporations will follow this lead and get their employees involved in mentoring and coaching.

"Ernst & Young employees are serving as guest speakers at workshops," she says. "But that's not all. In Calgary, they've started organizing monthly sessions at Ernst & Young's offices; they bring a group of kids into their offices, and they give them

175

pizza and tour them around, and talk about their industry as well as talking about a topic like budgeting for post-secondary studies. They've trained at least 150 Ernst & Young employees across the country, and so far the partnership has served close to 8,500 youths and adults across the country."

The Canadian Post-Secondary Access Partnership also managed to draw in aboriginal organizations in Saskatchewan and British Columbia as well as small-town schools in places like Biggar, Saskatchewan. The partnership has two websites (www.youcango.ca and www.accesspartnership.ca) and in Quebec it has collaborated with school commissions in an online advising service (www.osezlesetudes.qc.ca). In the fall of 2009, it convened an inaugural conference in Toronto called Prepared Minds, Prepared Places. The organizers planned a major push on social networking sites like Facebook and Twitter to attract attention to the issue of access and to the growing array of facilities aimed at helping people find their way to a satisfying experience of higher education.

And, says Diana Wickham, the other components of the vanishing Foundation were also taking their place in the mix. Laureates from the Excellence Awards Program were emerging as volunteers for the partnership's programs. The programs offered by the partnership had almost all grown out of the Foundation's research findings. The proposed research centre at the University of Victoria would help the partnership test the effectiveness of its activities. The components of the Foundation would echo throughout the partnership.

THE WORLD Petroleum Council bursaries ended with the Foundation. By the end of 2009, the Foundation had distributed 1,619 WPC Scholarships valued at $4.8 million. Several options

176

for the remaining funds, approximately $300,000, are still being evaluated, including the possibility of a joint project with the Canadian Post-Secondary Access Partnership.

Another possibility, says Randolf Harrold, would be to put the money into scholarships that would allow senior undergraduates with an interest in the industry to attend industry conferences. In 2008, for instance, the Foundation itself sponsored an essay contest for WPC recipients, with the winners being funded as youth members of the Canadian delegation to that year's World Petroleum Congress in Madrid, Spain. The heady experience of participating in plenary sessions, workshops and informal conversations with oil ministers, CEOs, engineers, geologists and financial analysts from Kazakhstan, Venezuela, Indonesia and Nigeria made a profound impression on the students. It is probably also true that the presence of eight hundred youth delegates from around the world—with their concerns about climate change, resource depletion, water pollution and security—made a profound impression on the industry.

The next congress will be held in Doha, Qatar, in 2011, and the choice of how to apply the funds will be largely up to the industry. But whichever option the industry chooses, says Randolf Harrold, "the remaining amount will be put to exciting initiatives with Canadian youth to attract and retain them in the industry."

177

NORMAN RIDDELL was sixty-five when the Foundation closed, and he had recently experienced a "heart episode"—not a heart attack, exactly, but an arterial blockage, angioplasty, a stent. So he's heading for retirement, right?

"No," he says, looking mildly indignant. "I hope I'm going to have something equally challenging to do after the Foundation's finished." He sits back, reflecting. "This was such a wonderful opportunity—two and a half billion dollars in the bank, and to work on something that's important. I'm very grateful to the board. I don't think I would have got the same enjoyment out of marketing toothpaste or something. This was *worth doing.*"

Stéphane LeBlanc and his wife are Acadians, from Shediac, New Brunswick, with a young son and two sets of doting grandparents back home. The pull is magnetic. He's had some interesting feelers about jobs in New Brunswick, and his severance package will allow him to move home, take a little time off and look for congenial work in the booming Moncton area.

For Melissa Moi, the end of the job at the Foundation is a glorious opportunity for her and her husband to live abroad for a while—maybe base themselves in Hong Kong for a few years.

"Losing your job when you're not even thirty yet is an opportunity and a kick in the butt to go and take a risk and try something really different," she says. "We don't have kids, we don't have any dependants, we don't have anything really holding us down in Canada. Five years before or five years from now I don't know if we'd have been willing to take this risk. We're excited—but it's really scary at the same time."

Chad Lubelsky may also travel or live abroad for "six months or a couple of years," but in his next job he'd like to travel less than he did with the Foundation. He's "grateful for the travel opportunities in that job, but I also know how destabilizing a lot of travel can be." He likes the idea of renting an apartment in Buenos Aires and perfecting his Spanish. But then he has parents in Montreal, so perhaps it would be as well to stay closer to home. He thinks he'd like to do a Ph.D. on "something to do with management, the role of relationships in leadership development and organizational development, maybe." Does that add up to trying to understand what he's learned about management during his time at the Foundation? Yes, it does.

He also wants to maintain the relationships he's developed in that job, not only with his colleagues but also with the marvellous young people he's worked with. They're fabulous, he says, and they're going to do great things. In fact, "I fully expect one of them to hire me some day."

Andrew Woodall thinks he may have rendered himself obsolete. A native Montrealer, he's had a remarkably satisfying career without ever having had to move away.

"I've been incredibly lucky up till now to do jobs that I've chosen and that have always given me a sense of learning and of personal development—and a huge sense that I'm helping to make the country and the world a better place," he reflects. "But I've worked with such great people that they do everything, so I can't really do anything myself any more. So what can I say I can do? I can motivate people. Yeah, great." He grins. But motivating people is a rare management skill, despite his self-deprecation.

"I know I want to work with leadership development, and I'd ideally like to work with the age group I've been dealing with, the kind of CEGEP-college-university age group. I've been focusing for the last seven or eight years on giving away other people's money." He laughs. "I really don't know what I'll do, but it's becoming increasingly imperative that I think about it more seriously."

Over his time at the Foundation, says Jean Lapierre, the voluntary commitments that he's seen through the Excellence Awards Program and elsewhere have made him want to be a volunteer himself.

"If I'm lucky, at the end of the process I may not have to work too much to earn a living," he says, and his work at the Foundation has made him passionate about the condition of aboriginal

Canadians. "So this is something I would like to give some time to. I have seen organizations, opportunities or initiatives that need professional support or help with communications. I've been doing it for now thirty-five years so I know a little bit about it. The idea of making this available for free is interesting.

"In my life I've seen many people who fight for initiatives, but they don't have money and because of that they don't go very far. But at one point it's not that you need money but you need strategies, you need professional advice. So I would like to start on a voluntary basis a communication firm that would advise freely people in organizations that have a social mission. I would like to gather a few of my friends in the same field and form a little group of professionals working free for people just because we think that we can help."

Interestingly, as the end approached, nobody in the Foundation seemed to be unduly fretful about the future. Nobody jumped ship early to take another job. Their calm focus on the work they were still doing expressed two things: confidence in their own abilities to find something satisfactory when the time came and absolute conviction that the job they were doing deserved their full attention until it was completed. It was, as Norman Riddell had said, *worth doing*.

FUNDAMENTALLY, THE Foundation was created to address the problem of access. It was also concerned with persistence and student debt, but those two can also be seen as aspects of access. And the basic reason that access is an issue for government is the labour market. To reiterate the key fact, in the knowledge economy, 80 per cent of the new jobs require some form of post-secondary education, but only 67 per cent of Canadians actually continue their education to the post-secondary level. If that percentage does not rise, Canada will find itself in the grotesque position of grappling simultaneously with employers who can't find workers and workers who can't find jobs.

This is a novel situation for a country that has always considered higher education to be the birthright of the elite and that always found work for most of its people in the forests, the mines and the fisheries. An economy that requires 80 per cent of its workforce to be educated really transforms the way we think about post-secondary education. We are now talking about post-secondary education for almost everyone, which means that we have to see it not just as university education, but as a broad spectrum of learning opportunities that includes colleges, private career institutions, apprenticeships, upgrading, continuing education, distance education and so on.

That broader vision of post-secondary education makes Foundation researcher Yves Pelletier think very hard about teacher education.

"You look at the Swedish model," he says. "In Sweden, anyone who has any form of post-secondary education can go to teachers' college and become a teacher. What does that mean, when you have someone who is actually college-trained in the classroom? The bias on universities disappears. When you have a good mixture of teachers who come from trades, who come from universities and colleges, you're not weakening the capacity, you're actually strengthening the diversity. I think that's one of the things that need to happen."

Ignoring for the moment the impact of the Foundation's programs on individuals, the Foundation's greatest achievement was probably its transformation of the way Canadians understand the concept of access to higher education and the barriers that keep people out. Its second greatest achievement was the

181

complementary demonstration that student aid is not just about money and that it can be tailored and targeted quite precisely to reach specific groups of Canadians who need it.

Its third great achievement was to give us, for the first time, an overview of the national educational system seen as a whole— and to demonstrate that it is a truly national educational system not only despite, but indeed because of, the fact that it consists of thirteen diverse provincial and territorial systems. Our educational system is not less national because it addresses the concerns of aboriginals on the Prairies, displaced fisheries workers on the Atlantic coast or redundant industrial workers in Ontario. What kind of a system would it be if it did *not* address the vital concerns of specific Canadians in their real social contexts?

"The unintended consequence of creating the Foundation," says Andrew Parkin, "was that you finally had an agency that was not part of all these different camps. It was federal, but it was independent of the federal government. It was not provincial, but it was partnering with the provinces. It was working with both college and university students, and what finally became very important is that, because it was working on access, it had to also think about students in the K–12 system.

"The people who created the Foundation never sat down and said, 'Well, what we need in this country is to think about education in an organization that is working both for the federal and provincial governments, college and university students and post-secondary and pre-post-secondary students.' They didn't think about that, but that's what we did. And often, when we were at meetings, everyone else was only talking about their own part of that system, and really the Foundation was the only body that talked about the whole. We talked about how federal and provincial programs interact, and we talked about the needs of different types of students because we were serving them all. It's not because we're better people. It's just that we were in a unique spot."

Allan Blakeney notes that the Foundation also provided a wholly voluntary bridge between the various provincial and territorial departments of education—and also served some groups who often fell between the cracks. The Foundation, he recalls, funded a conference on Inuit education, "and that may or may not pay off, but you've got to start somewhere, and there was nobody else to do it."

The Foundation also provided an innovative example of a mechanism for dealing with issues that seem exceptionally difficult for elected governments to handle—long-term issues, issues that need attention well beyond the length of an electoral cycle, or even two or three electoral cycles. The inability of governments to deal intelligently with such issues is a tragic failing in a period marked by long-term, often subtle concerns like climate change, cultural support, peak oil, globalization, the declining vitality of democracy itself and so forth.

Many of these are what might be called consensus issues— issues where we differ about means, not ends. Everyone, for instance, is in favour of less crime, more prosperity, less pollution, better health. The political debate is about how to reach such objectives, not about the objectives themselves. By the same token, nobody would deny that a better-educated population would be a good thing, and in a sense, the Foundation came to serve as a national advisory council that provided empirical evidence about the most effective ways to develop an educated population. One could make a case for other organizations devoted to doing research and developing policy on other long-term consensus issues.

Even as a ghost, the Foundation nudges the way we think.

LESSONS LEARNED

· · · · · · ·

"**D**O ME a favour," said the August Personage (having read about as much of this book as you have). "Insert a chapter that lists the lessons learned. I do some lecturing on public policy and public administration, and I think there are some valuable lessons that could be explicitly abstracted from this story. But we need to have the lessons pulled out and set off by themselves."

A Learned Professor of political science had a similar reaction, remarking that the Foundation came across as a kind of "skunkworks," to use a term popularized by management guru Tom Peters—"fast moving, informal, adaptive, information hungry, ready to try new things." He wondered why the Foundation had evolved that way. Was that a reflection of the characters of the key people? Or was it some combination of having a lot of money, very little time, a relatively manageable accountability procedure and an orientation towards getting results?

These questions are important, said the Learned Professor, because the Foundation "comes across as the kind of place governments often say they want to foster, but almost never do. If it happened in this case for reasons that could be replicated, there might be a lesson there for future government policy."

Norman Riddell never uses the word "skunkworks," but the concept explains why he vigorously rejects the contention that the Foundation was "brutally understaffed." A successful skunkworks has to be small to stay focused on results and to avoid becoming preoccupied with administrative process. Indeed, Riddell wonders whether the Foundation ultimately wasn't slightly *over*staffed.

Hmmm ... Would a separate chapter discussing such matters actually fit within the concept of the book? Maybe, maybe not. What sorts of lessons did the August Personage want to isolate?

"Well," said the August Personage, "I'm thinking about things like the force of personality and the importance of the individual. You talk about Jean Monty or Norman Riddell or Alex Usher or Andrew Parkin and the impact that they had on the Foundation. You make the point quite forcefully in several places that this thing would have been very different if it hadn't been for the contributions of these individuals—and that's obviously right.

"There's a real lesson in here that you can't abstract the policy or the program delivery from the individuals who are involved. That's a big lesson, I can tell you, because most people think that this stuff takes place in a vacuum. But if somebody puts on his pants in the morning and has a fight with his wife before he goes to work, it affects the design of the program. We tend to think that a program is what it is, and it doesn't matter who shapes it or delivers it. But that does matter."

The August Personage went on to note that effective government work requires real drive and determination, a point that is not well appreciated either by scholars or by the general public. Indeed, a widespread cynicism about government makes it difficult for that perception to gain any traction. But the faceless bureaucrats have real personalities, and the people who do good government work are people of character. He also noted the importance of teams as well as individuals and the impact of a team's chemistry on the success or failure of the program.

"Another thing to take away from this story," he said, "is that there are so many gems like this that are just completely unknown. We know all about the failures. Those we talk about. But you only do post-mortems where there's a body. No body, no post-mortem. So the successes go unrecognized. You know, all across the country today—this very day—public servants did wonderful things for Canadians and nobody noticed. Well, that's generally the objective in the public service: to be taken for granted. But it's an important learning from this, to realize that there are many government activities that we don't hear about precisely because they're actually working very well."

The August Personage drew a whole series of additional lessons, like the need for a national perspective even in areas of provincial jurisdiction. Every citizen of a province is also a citizen of Canada, and the way that governments serve that citizen needs to reflect the unity as well as the duality of that citizenship. A perfect illustration is the issue of displacement, which vexed the Foundation throughout its life, whereby the provinces tend to vacate areas in which the feds are spending money. Norman Riddell came to believe that the only way to avoid that problem was to stop running separate and parallel programs. Organize joint federal–provincial programs, and the problem disappears.

And, says the August Personage, if the Foundation's history illustrates the sometimes-crippling difficulties inherent in

Canada's federal structure, it also shows the creative possibilities of a flexible approach to federalism that includes a willingness to honour the particularities of different provinces. "Asymmetrical federalism" has real advantages.

Another lesson, said the August Personage, is that it's sometimes in the public interest to keep your activities off the radar screen. You can do a lot of good by stealth. At the beginning, when the environment was hostile, the Foundation benefitted from a communications policy that consisted of not communicating much at all.

"I'm also reminded of the importance of 'not invented here' as a policy criterion," he said. In government, an idea's origins greatly affect its perceived merit. In this case, "the Foundation was Prime Minister Chrétien's idea. The provinces, the bureaucrats and Mr. Chrétien's successors would all have liked it a lot better if it had been *their* idea."

And the value of year-end money—un-earmarked, unallocated—is precisely that it affords the opportunity for a government (or just a prime minister) to do something imaginative and unique, outside the usual constraints of intergovernmental relationships, established budgetary priorities and departmental expectations. The Foundation shows that such an organization can be self-governing, very effective and fully respectful of Parliament.

188   The Foundation's history, said the August Personage, provided a powerful demonstration of the role of analysis and research in policy and program development, which was one of the initial weaknesses of the Foundation. As Norman Riddell says, "I wish I had known at the beginning what I know now. We've acquired an understanding of how the design of student financial assistance affects behaviour and of how money has to

be supplemented with other kinds of initiatives if it's to achieve the objectives, but what we knew about these subjects at the beginning was next to nothing. If we had known, or if we had had a longer period to do research, we might not have organized the program the way we did it. We might well have organized it in the way we eventually did it. But when you're supposed to be doing a Millennium project, you can hardly wait till 2005 to do it."

The Learned Professor, says Riddell, has "speculated quite correctly" about some of the factors that made the Foundation an effective skunkworks. The pressure to get things done in a very short period of time was a major factor, creating a pre-occupation with results. In addition, the wide range of people recruited by the Foundation brought their own creativity and drive, and they identified personally with the mission—a charac-teristic "facilitated by the relative lack of rules and regulations."

Riddell also points out two little-noted benefits of the Foun-dation model. First, it was able to enter into a whole variety of pilot projects with individual provinces to test programs on a small scale, something that the government itself would never be able to do. Second, although the Foundation was endowed with $2.5 billion, it actually delivered $3.3 billion in public goods—$800 million more than it cost the government.

For Riddell, it was also important that the Foundation was not tied closely to the political level, so it could evaluate its programs honestly, face up to its errors, redesign the failed programs and try again. In a way, it was as much like a pri-vate company as a government department. When Ford made the Edsel and it flopped, the company regrouped and produced something else without having to worry about a whole pack of Parliamentarians baying for its minister to resign.

But the distance from the political level was also a problem for the Foundation, particularly when the time came for renewal, because it had no political leader—no minister, specifically—to speak for it. Other parts of government can command public attention in that way—but a para-public organization like the Foundation has no political voice.

The Learned Professor nods. In a sense, he says, the Foundation was a political failure. It had no political support in Ottawa, and it did not meet the objectives of its founder. Yes, Chrétien "wanted to do some good things for higher education, but he also wanted to get credit and visibility for the federal government. He didn't really get it." The Learned Professor argues that once the Foundation became focused on its intricate minuets with the provinces, its relationship with the federal government faded in importance. It could even be argued that its cordial relationships with the provinces were achieved, in part, at the expense of its relationship with Ottawa.

All of which shows, says Norman Riddell, "how difficult it is to be a friend to Ottawa and the provinces at the same time." Riddell recognizes that the federal government may have been disappointed that the Foundation did not generate the visibility it had hoped for. But, he says, Mr. Chrétien had also noted that student debt had doubled in the previous ten years, and he wanted to change that. Student debt flattened during the ten years of the Foundation's existence, so "if that's what he was after, he got it."

"One of the most powerful themes that comes out of this story," says the August Personage, "is the transformative power of education. The anecdotes and examples express that very strongly, and I think it's a fantastic reminder of just what the government was trying to do in the first place."

He's right. This is a story about change, and the most important of all the changes are the ones that transform students and make them more imaginative, more competent, more self-confident, more fit and willing to play a major role in a country that already belongs to them. Agreed.

"Good," says the August Personage. "So: do you think there's room in the book for a chapter like the one I'm proposing? Lessons learned, explicitly stated? Ruminations and reflections by scholars and practitioners? That sort of thing?"

Oh no, my friend, I'm afraid not. There isn't any place in this book for a chapter like that.

› The Foundation's Descendants

. . . .

"THESE AREN'T *Canada's future leaders. These are leaders in Canada right now.*"

Students graduate, go out into the world and begin to make their contribution. Right?

In general, perhaps. But some students commence their contributions long before graduation. Sometimes students lever their post-secondary studies to advance the causes they've already adopted. They discern opportunities for change everywhere—in their admission to university, their selection as scholarship winners, their eligibility for project grants—and they seize every opportunity to amplify their influence. They do not merely intend to change the world. They are changing the world already, and graduation simply opens the door to the next opportunity.

"I STARTED my business when I was fourteen, in Grade 9," says Ben Barry. "My company was focused on trying to challenge status quo beauty and to create a fashion industry that celebrates beauty that's authentic, beauty that's in everyone—and that really works to empower and develop positive self-esteem."

The idea sprang from Ben's indignation at the experience of a friend from his Ottawa high school who had taken a modelling course and had been told that if she wanted to work as a model she'd have to change her appearance, particularly by losing some weight.

"I thought she was beautiful, and she should be able to model, and she shouldn't have to change herself," Ben remembers. "So I started to send off her picture to magazines and local companies in the city, and started getting phone calls back from people that wanted to hire her, and assumed that I was her agent. And I thought, Sure! Why not?"

With the help of friends from Child and Youth-Friendly Ottawa (CAYFO), a local youth organization, he organized a charity fundraising fashion show on Parliament Hill "to celebrate beauty in all different cultures and all different sizes and all different backgrounds, and to challenge people's notions of beauty." Through CAYFO, other young people approached him to ask for help in establishing their own businesses while staying in school—a magazine, a landscaping business, a snow-clearing service, a jewellery kiosk in the Ottawa market.

Meanwhile, his first model was delighted that Ben had found work for her, and she suggested he try to find more. He did, and she began sending him other friends who wanted to model. He found himself hanging between the two worlds of fashion and high school—and making some interesting links between them.

"In the fashion industry, I was learning about the strict criteria they have for models and their narrow idea of beauty—and in my other role, I was in high school with my friends, and I was also seeing that my friends and family certainly didn't look like the models in all of the ads. In fact, looking at these models day after day was negatively impacting their sense of themselves. The culture is so visual. You have images on the Internet, in

magazines, on billboards, on buses, on university campuses—
and every image is essentially the same. So inevitably that one
ideal seeps into your system.

"So the idea I've always had with my company is that I just
wanted to have my friends and their families represented. We're
not trying to replace one ideal with another. What I wanted to
see was body variety and age variety and cultural background
variety, so that you see a plethora of different shapes and forms
and sizes and ages and backgrounds represented in the images."

After high school, Ben Barry got a Millennium scholarship
and headed off to the University of Toronto to study business. He
quickly realized that he already knew a good deal about business and thought he should broaden his horizons by studying
something else. He chose women's studies, and it was "the best
decision possible. It changed the whole way I thought about my
business."

He concluded that it was not healthy for his models to work
full-time as models, because in modelling "they're solely valued
for how they look. And in fact they're more successful and more
creative when they bring their varied life experiences to bear on
their modelling. So the models we represent are artists, students,
lawyers, teachers, entrepreneurs, and we really encourage them
to reveal their personalities and their character and their attitude in their work."

194 Does this remind you of the striking variety of beautiful and
varied women in the Dove soap Campaign for Real Beauty? Yes?
No wonder. Ben Barry consulted with Ogilvy & Mather, the
advertising agency behind that campaign, and also provided
some of the models. And how did the campaign succeed in the
marketplace? Within the first six months after the first install-
ment, Dove's sales increased by 700 per cent.

Which proves that the consumer is ready for a different approach to modelling and beauty, right?

Well, maybe. Other companies and agencies remained wary. The Dove campaign, they said, was a fluke. It worked because it was the first such campaign. It would never work for us. There's no empirical research to support this wacko notion that consumers will respond well to models who reflect humanity's glorious diversity.

So Ben set out to conduct that research. He signed up for an M.Phil at Cambridge University, graduating in 2007. Today, he's running focus groups and surveys in six countries—Canada, the U.S., the U.K., China, India and Brazil. He's testing "whether viewing models of the age, size and cultural background of the consumer increases purchase intentions more than using a model that reflects the current Western beauty ideal." When he's done, he'll have a Ph.D. from Cambridge.

And what about the modelling agency, which is itself a test of his ideas about beauty? It has grown to employ thirty people in its Toronto head office. It represents more than three hundred models—all of them beautiful, every one unique.

Ben Barry spends three months in England and one month in Toronto, running both the research project and the company from his laptop. You have to learn how to delegate, he says. You have to learn how to pick people and then trust them. That's "the only way to grow and to ever move from a one- or two-person operation to a sustainable venture."

He's been running and growing his leading-edge modelling agency for twelve years now. He's twenty-six years old.

MARIE-RENÉE BERGERON-LAJOIE is like a fireworks display—beautiful, brilliant, exploding with energy and light. A native of Shawinigan and the daughter of an electrical contractor, she grew up in Romania and Haiti as well as Quebec. At seventeen, she spent her summer working in a health centre in Peru's Amazon basin, doing blood tests, picking up Spanish and trying out the idea that she might want to study medicine. She loved it: "If I could do this all my life, I'd be the most happiest person!" She was an athlete and an impresario, bringing *The Vagina Monologues* to Trois-Rivières, where she attended the local CEGEP. She was valedictorian at the college, but she had to miss her own graduation in order to attend her first Think Again conference in Ottawa. Then she was off to study medicine at McGill.

She used her Millennium Project Grant to work with Dr. Gilles Julien, a "social pediatrician" working in the poorest districts of Montreal. Social pediatrics is based on the U.N. Convention on the Rights of the Child, and Dr. Julien has brought together a team of doctors, nurses, social workers and others, so that when a child appears at his clinic with something like delayed development or ADHD or some other condition, the team looks at the child in his or her social context, networking with the schools and the public health services to try to provide for the child's needs within a framework much broader than what traditional medicine provides.

"His clinic is a kitchen table," says Marie-Renée. "He brings in children, grandparents, friends, people involved in this child's care. He's done many things in Quebec to challenge our vision of what is health care and how are we treating our children. It really changed my view of medicine. Very inspiring for me—a model of practising medicine which revolves around community, around commitment and around respecting one another as individuals."

With five other fellow medical students, Marie-Renée established a group called Sexperts, aimed at combatting a rising incidence of sexually transmitted diseases among teenagers

196

in Quebec—chlamydia, gonorrhea, even syphilis. The most affected group was between the ages of twenty and twenty-four, but "we know those habits begin when you're much younger, thirteen or fifteen. So what can we do as medical students? We thought we'd create a peer-education program where we'd create interactive activities for high schools to get teenagers to think about these things. We weren't saying, 'Don't have sex'; we weren't saying, 'Do have sex.' We were just saying, 'You'll take the decision at the right time for you, but you'll have all the resources around you that can make a difference if something goes wrong.'

"So we started taking these things out to high schools—and *bing!* It caught fire! The high schools loved it, and we created a training program and a binder full of all the activities, and we expanded it over into French at Université de Montréal, and then it spread to Quebec City, at Université Laval—and now the project has over two hundred medical students presenting around the province."

She pauses to reflect about the scale of the problem.

"For me, it was heartbreaking to see those teenagers who actually believe we have a cure for AIDS, or think that if you're sick you're going to see it—you know, if you get gonorrhea the symptoms will be gross. Well, no, they might not be. Now we're getting statistics from the States telling us that a third of infertility cases actually result from untreated infections. And when do those things happen? At thirteen, fifteen, twenty—and maybe they never even know they had a disease, because a third of cases are asymptomatic.

"So we're very proud of this, and we're training more students. Sexperts is starting now at Sherbrooke and also at Trois-Rivières and Chicoutimi. We've worked a bit with the International Federation of Medical Students' Associations because there are a few projects like this that have emerged in other countries. And I actually had the opportunity to present—so lucky!—at a meeting in Canterbury, England, on what we've done here, and we shared our material with a few other countries who wanted to develop something similar."

An incredible achievement for half a dozen undergraduates.

"Being a doctor is caring for people," says Marie-Renée, with a smile like a burst of sunlight. "And the ethics and ideas we develop today will drive the future."

WHEN YOU'RE talking to child soldiers in Liberia, says Paul Cormier, the most important thing is simply your presence. Just the fact that you've come to sit with them and listen to them.

Paul is the national president of an anti-genocide organization called SHOUT (Students Helping Others Understand Tolerance), which has branches on more than twenty Canadian campuses. SHOUT's mandate is to create awareness of the specific issue of genocide, and its complementary mandate is the creation of dialogue between mutually suspicious groups— bringing together diverse campus groups like Christian, Jewish and Muslim organizations, for example, and staging a dialogue. SHOUT is not an international development organization, but it does organize educational trips abroad—to Poland and Germany to visit the concentration camps, to Rwanda to visit the sites of the 1994 genocide, to Washington to visit museums and make political contacts there.

But Paul Cormier's real passion is international development. He spent two summers doing development work in Haiti, and afterward "I looked at my university, and we have a series of international exchange opportunities, but they were to universities in Texas and Australia and Europe. There were no educational trips to the developing world, and I thought that was a void in the university that needed to be addressed, so that's why I started Students for West Africa. All the Students for West Africa team were part of the executive of the Fredericton branch of SHOUT."

Students for West Africa was a sub-program of Forum for Education in West Africa, a partnership of twenty universities in West Africa and twenty universities in the West that involves exchanges of people, technology and educational resources. Students for West Africa was designed to be the vehicle for student participation in the program.

"We wanted to go there and listen, to not go there with preconceived notions of what these people need, and then to come home and educate and create awareness in our own communities," Paul says. "As a side note, that's something that the Millennium really helped with, because one of the main things about the Millennium Project Grants is that the trip itself isn't the end result. The real result is what happens when you come back and what you do with your life, how the trip changes you and how you change the community you're in."

Students for West Africa took seven students from New Brunswick—from St. Thomas University and University of New Brunswick—to Guinea, Mali and Liberia. Three of the students worked in Guinea on vitamin distribution and in agriculture. Two students worked in health care in Mali. Paul himself went to Liberia with a partner, Elizabeth, to work with child soldiers and with street kids.

"The civil war ended in 2005, but Liberia is by no means peaceful," Paul says. "I was working in a slum in the ghetto known as Solalie, which means 'death is better than life,' which tells you the mentality that these kids experience every day. I think that the number one thing that I could offer these kids is 'presence,' just to sit and listen to them. They were blown away by the idea of someone of my background going to sit with them and trying to understand what they're going through. I never will really understand, but the fact that I extended my hand in friendship really moved them."

The first time Paul visited the ghetto, one of the kids told him that he was the first white person ever to visit there. Liberia has plenty of aid organizations, but the few that work with street kids tend to take the kids out of the ghetto to attend programs and then send them back. Paul's approach was to go into the ghettos and slums, get to know the kids and their needs and then bring officials into the slums to meet the kids in their own context.

"I would take them there into the ghettos with me so that they could see the actual conditions that the kids are living in," he says. "A team of health officials would meet the kids there in the ghetto, living in the bamboo structures or the boxcar, and see the twelve-year-old doing heroin, or see the kids all smoking pot . . . with tuberculosis or malaria or HIV/AIDS. They could see these things, and that really fostered compassion, fostered understanding."

The experience had a profound influence on Paul Cormier. Indeed, it reshaped his ambitions for the future.

"I'm going to study international human rights law next year for a master's program in Galway, Ireland, at University College Galway," he says. "I hope to pursue human rights law on an international level, but my actual dream or passion would be to create a series of intake programs for street kids internationally. Because street kids are forgotten internationally." .

THE BEN Barry Agency. Sexperts. Students for West Africa.

"These aren't Canada's future leaders. These are leaders in Canada right now."

seven

A MILLION FUTURES

· · · · · · ·

THE GULF Stream takes shape in the Caribbean
Sea, carrying tropical warmth and the seeds
of palm trees northward through the Straits of
Florida and on up the Atlantic coast. Off Newfoundland it turns
eastward, crosses the ocean and confers upon the western tips of
the British Isles—County Cork, Cornwall, the Hebrides—a climate so warm that the palm seeds take root and grow.

And then, in the Arctic, the stream is chilled, and its waters
sink to the bottom, turn southward and flow unseen until they
well up again in the Southern Ocean, off Antarctica. The current is no longer visible, but it is still part of the ocean, part of
the great circulation that makes life possible on this planet.

Perhaps the impact of the Canada Millennium Scholarship
Foundation is like that. For a time, it was extremely visible, and
its impacts were obvious and sometimes dramatic. Now it sinks
from view—but its influence continues, invisible yet profound.

Only 33 million people live in Canada, and the Foundation distributed more than a million bursaries and

scholarships—1,067,035, to be exact. That's more than one scholarship for every thirty-three Canadians. Indeed, for the segment of the population most affected by the Foundation's activities, those between eighteen and thirty years of age, the proportion would be more like one scholarship or bursary for every ten such Canadians.

A million investments in the future of our young people and of the country. You might as well say a million futures nourished by the nation.

The energy liberated by those investments will flow subtly through the depths of our national life. The effects will not be obvious, but they will be significant. Former students, members of the Millennium Alumni Network, enriching communities across the country. Turned-on teachers in Chilliwack and Shediac. A flow of research reports from the University of Victoria. Immigrants and school dropouts at the local YMCA slowly coming to believe that they, too, can go to college and forge a better future for their children.

An oil-patch executive who was once a World Petroleum Congress Scholar arguing in a boardroom that the corporation really needs to join the Canadian Post-Secondary Access Partnership. A judge, remembering the award that got her through law school, giving a suspended sentence to a surly teenager—on condition that the teen report to the career counselling centre to explore the possibility of taking up a trade. A concerto by a young composer from the Yukon who had never heard an orchestra until he got a scholarship and went away to school.

And a huge new bursary program coming out of Ottawa.

What remains of the Canada Millennium Scholarship Foundation in our national life is a long-submerged wave train initiated by an organization that truly loved those who craved learning, an organization that truly loved aspiration and determination and excellence, and a corps of young people who therefore knew their country well and had reason to love it deeply.

It's gone, that organization. It's gone. But it's everywhere.

> ACKNOWLEDGEMENTS

· · · · · · ·

A GREAT MANY people contributed to the process that brought this book into existence, and I am grateful to all of them.

First, I am grateful to Norman Riddell and his management group at the Canada Millennium Scholarship Foundation for asking me to submit a proposal to write this book, and then for accepting the proposal. I am particularly grateful to Jean Lapierre, the Foundation's communications director and my main liaison with the organization, who has been an absolute pleasure to work with.

Because my work was supported by the Foundation, I am not receiving royalties from the sales of this book. Those funds will instead be contributed to the Lulu Terrio-Cameron Memorial Scholarship Fund at Cape Breton University (CBU). All the research materials, notes and other working papers from the project will also go to CBU, where they will be deposited in the Cape Breton Archives.

The staff of the Foundation have been unfailingly helpful and considerate. Many of them had already been interviewed at length by Dr. Rosemary Reilly of Concordia University, and they submitted very cheerfully to further interviews by me—and in some cases, notably Andrew Parkin and Andrew Woodall, to more than one interview, as well as to repeated phone calls and emails. Several former Foundation employees, especially Alex Usher and Franca Gucciardi, were extremely helpful, as were the Foundation members, past and present. I am particularly grateful to the Foundation's former chairman, Gérard Veilleux, for his generosity and candour.

I was welcomed by several participants in the Foundation's research programs, notably Stan Watchorn, Yvonne Rondeau and the Babin family, and by Foundation volunteers like Peter Wong. I was fortunate to have the full cooperation of former senior civil servants who had been influential in shaping the Foundation at the outset, especially Robert Bourgeois and Mel Cappe, and with well-placed observers like the August Personage. I also had the benefit of discussions with present and former provincial student aid officials such as Tom Glenwright in Manitoba and Kevin Chapman in Nova Scotia.

Don Sedgwick, the project's literary agent, genially harassed me into producing a convincing proposal for publishers and skillfully negotiated a complex three-way publishing contract between me, the Foundation and Canada's largest independently owned publishing house, Douglas & McIntyre. A draft of the manuscript was read by two trusted advisers with long experience in public service, namely my brothers Ken and David, and also by Mel Cappe, Nigel Chippindale, the Learned Professor and the August Personage. My heartiest thanks go to all of them. And I'm grateful to Peter Norman, my editor at Douglas & McIntyre, for his dedication to clarity, accuracy and rhythm.

My deepest gratitude, though, is reserved for my beloved wife, most gifted editor and best friend, Marjorie Simmins, and for the many students I met in the course of this project. Some of the students' stories appear in the book, though many do not— but Marjorie notes that she always knew when I'd been having a heart-to-heart interview with a student because I invariably came downstairs from my workroom beaming with delight and bursting to talk. Canada is blessed to have a phenomenal cohort of brilliant, dedicated, brave and imaginative young people just coming into bloom. It has been a great privilege to get to know some of them.

⟩ INDEX

· · · · · · ·